June, 1996

 ® Clearinghouse on Information & Technology
Syracuse University

Syracuse, New York
IR-102

Helping with Homework:
A Parent's Guide to Information Problem-Solving

This publication is available from Information Resources Publications, Syracuse University, 4-194 Center for Science and Technology, Syracuse, New York 13244-4100; 1-800-464-9107 (IR-102)

ISBN: 0-937597-42-2

This publication is prepared with funding from the Office of Educational Research and Improvement, U.S. Department of Education, under contract no. RR93002009. The opinions expressed in this report do not necessarily reflect the positions or policies of OERI or ED.

Eric Plotnick, Editor in Chief
Susann L. Wurster, Copy Editor

Helping with homework :
 a parent's guide to
    9-25-2000   SDW

e Authors

Michael B. Eisenberg is director of the ERIC Clearinghouse on Information and Technology and the award-winning AskERIC service. His work focuses on the use of information and information technology by individuals and organizations to meet their information needs and manage their information more effectively and efficiently. Mike is a full professor at Syracuse University's School of Information Studies teaching at all levels, undergraduate through Ph.D. He conducts research, writes, consults, and lectures frequently on information problem-solving, information technology, the Internet, and information management in learning and teaching.

Mike is a graduate of State University of New York at Albany (B.A. and M.L.S.). He earned a certificate of advanced studies and a Ph.D. in information transfer from Syracuse University.

Michael B. Eisenberg

Robert E. Berkowitz is library media specialist at Wayne Central High School (Ontario Center, NY). Bob has successfully managed school libraries for Head Start-12th grade in both rural and urban settings. He has been an educational professional since 1971. Bob is a strong believer in active, curriculum-centered library media programs and promotes the integration of information literacy skills across the entire curriculum. He consults with state education departments, school districts and local schools. He also shares his ideas at state, regional, and local conferences and seminars. Bob is an adjunct professor at Syracuse University's School of Information Studies and has taught at other institutions of higher education.

Bob's degrees include: B.A. from American International College (Springfield, MA.); M.A. in Education, George Washington University; M.L.S. State University of New York at Albany; and School Administrator's Certification, North Adams State College (North Adams, MA.).

Robert E. Berkowitz

Table of Contents

Chapter 3   55

Chapter 4   65

List of Figures

List of Appendices

To our children—
Brian, Laura, Adam, and Marette—
who taught us how to help with homework.

Helping with Homework

A Parent's Guide to Information Problem Solving

This book is about helping kids succeed in whatever they choose to do. It's about parents being able to do more than simply providing a quiet place

for their children to study and urging them to do their homework. It's about tried and tested ways of working with kids of all ages to help them complete tasks and solve problems.

Parents Helping Children: The Challenge

We all know that parents can play an important role in helping their children succeed. There is a wide body of research (including the 1994 United States Department of Education report, *Strong Families, Strong Schools*) that shows that parents can make a difference in their children's learning. There is evidence that helping children with home-based work in particular can enhance the learning process.

This is very encouraging, however few parents know how to help in meaningful ways. They try hard, but even their best efforts can result in disappointment and conflict rather than in satisfaction and success.

That's what we address in this book—how parents can help their children in meaningful and satisfying ways that result in success. Our goal is simple but powerful:

> **to give parents an effective approach and the tools they need
> to help their children learn and achieve.**

We believe that parents can work in meaningful ways to help their children learn and do well in school. Many researchers agree that homework fosters student initiative and responsibility. But homework and assignments can do much more than that. Homework and assignments can provide opportunities for children to learn how to complete tasks and solve problems. And parents can help to see that this happens.

Wherever students turn, they're faced with answering questions, writing reports, and creating projects. Most of these assignments require work beyond the school day. Homework and student assignments provide excellent opportunities for parent-student connections.

Our Approach: The Big Six

Most books about helping children with school stress good study habits, a quiet study area, and managing time. We certainly agree with these recommendations, but we believe that parents can do even more. Parents can help their children by guiding them through an information problem-solving process called *the Big Six*.

The Big Six process applies to all kinds of school work—homework, assignments, projects, reports, and even tests. For students, the Big Six provides a familiar, tried and tested approach to completing their work. For parents, the Big Six provides numerous opportunities for them to ask the right questions and to guide their children in helpful ways.

Although well-meaning, many parents often don't know the best ways to help their children with school work. Frequently, parents wind up struggling or in outright conflict with their kids about how to do something. Parents need to pick the right time and offer appropriate types of assistance, or the results can be disastrous. For example, does the following sound familiar?

Laura and her father are working on math problems. He is trying to show her how to do a long division problem. She is getting frustrated and yells, "That's wrong; that's not the way my teacher does it!" He tries to explain that there are different ways to get to the correct answer and this way is easy and has worked for him for years. But Laura won't listen, and she finally storms off saying she will do it herself.

It's important that parents strive hard to avoid this type of confrontation.

In our opinion, the key to helping students succeed lies in the process of helping them, but not doing the work for them or trying to teach them. Leave teaching to the teachers and the work to the students. A better role for parents is to provide guidance and assistance, making it easier for children to succeed. The Big Six provides a workable framework for providing meaningful guidance.

Technology: A Valuable Tool

Adding to the burden for parents is pressure related to today's new technologies. Is it essential for my child to have a computer at home? If we already have a computer, is it good enough? What about the Internet, multimedia, and CD-ROMs? And, how can I help my child with all these things if I don't know how to use them myself?

Computers fit nicely into the Big Six process. Too often, computers and related technologies are presented as solutions in search of problems. For students and parents, it is helpful to view computers as tools that expand our ability to do things. For example, when building a house, it's quicker and easier to use an electric saw to cut pieces of wood. So too, when writing a report, it's quicker and easier to use word processing on a computer to organize and present information. In both of these examples, if the technology is used effectively, it will result in more accurate and improved final products.

Through guidance, parents can help students use technology in meaningful ways. For example, by asking the right questions, parents can help students recognize when and how various computer capabilities might be applied. Parents can also assist by arranging access for their children to computers and related software (through school, libraries, community agencies, or at home).

The challenge for parents, then, is to know how to guide their children, to know what questions to ask them, and to know when to do so. The Big Six approach to information problem-solving provides a valuable framework for meeting this challenge.

Overview of the Book

This book focuses on various strategies that parents can use to help their children succeed. The Big Six framework is the key. We explain all strategies in terms of the Big Six. Each chapter focuses on one aspect of the challenges facing students and parents:

Chapter 1: The Big Six Approach: A Framework for Helping Children
Chapter 2: What Your Children Face Every Day in School: Assignments
Chapter 3: The Big Six Applied: A Framework for Helping Children
           With Homework

Chapter 4: Computers, the Internet and Other Technologies: Can They
          Really Make a Difference?
Chapter 5: Assisting with Assignments: Examples from Various Subjects
Chapter 6: Bringing It All Together: A Parent Conversation with Mike
          and Bob

Our purpose is to help parents become partners in their children's success
in school by offering them practical ways to help with homework and assignments. Every parent can help to some degree. Even if you weren't
personally "a star" in school, you can still help your children. Your first
step is to accept the role of a guide, not a teacher. Your second step is to
learn how to ask questions that will help your kids work through the Big
Six process.

Summary

In this introduction, we presented a model that parents can use to help
their children learn and succeed. Let's summarize the key points:

(1) Parent/adult involvement is important to student learning.
(2) Parents can make a difference by helping, not teaching or doing.
(3) The Big Six provides parents with a practical framework for
    guiding students.
(4) Technology is a powerful tool—within Big Six context.
(5) All parents can help their children—even if they weren't great
    successes in school themselves.

1

The Big Six Approach

A Framework for Helping Children

In this chapter, we will explain the Big Six approach in detail. We will focus on the specifics of the Big Six and give you some practical examples of ways you can use the Big Six immediately to help your children succeed.

For many years, we have worked with students, teachers, and school librarians to develop students' information problem-solving abilities using an approach called the Big Six. The Big Six is a set of skills that is transferable to school, personal, and work applications. It is applicable to all subject areas across the full range of grade levels. Students can use the Big Six Skills whenever they need information to solve a problem, make a decision, or complete a task.

Parents can best assist their children by acting as guides and helpers. The Big Six Skills approach provides parents with a strategy to use as they fulfill this role. When tackling an assignment, parents can walk their kids through the process by asking key questions and focusing students' attention on specific actions to accomplish. By guiding students through the Big Six problem-solving process, parents can help them be more successful. This can all be done in a reasonable amount of time, with a reasonable amount of effort, and a maximum amount of results.

Focusing on the Process: The Super Three

The most important thing about the Big Six is that it is a process. There's a natural and logical flow from the beginning of a task through the various activities that lead to completion of that task. In fact, when we work with very young children (kindergarten and first grade), we often talk about the "Super Three" before we introduce the Big Six. The Super Three consists of:

BEGINNING   Plan what you are going to do.

MIDDLE   Do it.

END   Review what you did.[1]

---

1. Please note that the "plan, do, review" model is not original to our work. While we haven't been able to identify its first use, it is found in a number of state and local curricula and in one of the Effective Schools frameworks.

In the beginning, when students receive an assignment or homework, they should first think:

- what am I supposed to do?
- what will the result look like if I do a really good job?
- what do I need to find out about to do the job?

In the middle, students complete the various activities. This includes finding the necessary resources, reading or viewing the information in the sources, and putting it all together as a finished assignment.

Finally, at the end, before the assignment is completely finished and turned in, students should again stop and think:

- is this done?
- did I do what I was supposed to do?
- do I feel OK about this?
- should I do something else before I turn it in?

That's the Super Three. It emphasizes the flow of the information process. It sounds like a story, and it is. In fact, this is one quick way for you to help your kids get started or find out where they might be having trouble.

To get kids started, ask them to tell you their story from the beginning, when they are first starting out with the assignment. What are they going to do? How are they going to get there? Do they see any difficult spots in advance? Do the kids really know what the finished product will look like?

To help trouble-shoot problems in the middle, ask your children to explain what they have done up to that point. Have they lost sight of their goal? Are they stuck in one particular place? What still lies ahead?

Finally, at the end, ask them to tell you the story about what they did, and
how well they did it. If they were to do it again, what would be different
in the story? What could they have done differently that would have made
it better? And please note that the kids don't always need to actually go
back and do it again. Recognizing how we would change things is sometimes enough. That's learning.

The Full Process:
The Big Six Approach to Information Problem-Solving

While the Super Three is a good way to begin thinking about the information process, we will need much more detail if we are to guide and
assist children in meaningful ways. That's where the Big Six comes in.
The Big Six approach is a step-by-step process for solving information
problems. It's applicable across many situations:

> *Whenever students are confronted with an information-based problem to
> solve—homework, assignment, test, quiz, or decision—they can use the Big
> Six approach.*

The Big Six

1. Task Definition: Define the problem.
                        Identify the information needed (type,
                        amount, format, etc.).

2. Information   Brainstorm all possible sources.
   Seeking Strategies: Select the best sources.

3. Location & Access: Locate sources.
                        Find information within sources.

4. Use of Information: Examine information in sources (read, hear, view).

Extract relevant information.

5. Synthesis: Organize information from multiple sources.

Present the result.

6. Evaluation: Judge the result (effectiveness).

Judge the process (efficiency).

In practice, we have found that each of these six stages is necessary for solving information problems. The stages do not necessarily need to be completed in order, nor are people always aware that they are engaging in a particular stage. Successful information problem-solving requires at some point however: defining the task selecting, locating, and using appropriate information sources; pulling the information together; and deciding that the task is in fact completed.

Let's take a closer look at each of the Big Six Skills:

Task Definition

Task Definition is the stage at which students determine what needs to be done and what information is needed to get the job done. We find that the number one problem situation students can have is not knowing what's expected of them. There are lots of reasons for this (kids not paying attention, teacher not clear, task is confusing). Regardless of reason, if your children don't understand what they are to do and don't understand the basis upon which their work will be graded, they are at a tremendous disadvantage.

Parents can help by bringing the task and the grading criteria into focus. Look at the assignment sheet or the questions. Ask what the teacher will be looking for when he or she is grading. Make sure the students truly understand what it is they are to do, and how the assignment will be evaluated.

There's a second part to task definition: determining the information requirements. Here, we are not talking about various resources (books, computer databases, magazines). They come later. Here, we want students to think about what types of information they will need to get the job done (facts, opinions, pictures, numerical information) and about how much information they will need.

Information Seeking Strategies

Once students understand the task or problem and have some idea about the types of information needed, their attention needs to turn to the range of possible information sources. This is the brainstorming stage—figuring out all possible information sources, and then selecting the sources that are most appropriate and available. Once they get into it, kids are generally quite good at brainstorming sources. Your goal is to get them to think broadly.

For example, when starting a report or project, students usually rely on the usual sources—books, reference materials, and magazines. Other resources may include local and regional topic experts. Students might greatly enhance their projects by consulting with these people. They might also use a broad range of computer sources. First they need to think broadly about all types of resources. They must then narrow and select those sources that really meet their needs in terms of richness of information and availability.

Parents can help by brainstorming with their children the wide range of possible resources, and then letting the students figure out which ones to check first, second, etc.

Location & Access

Location & Access should be the easiest stage, but it often isn't. It's also not a very exciting or particularly interesting stage. But, it does need to be completed if your children are to succeed.

The goal in this stage is to locate the sources selected under the Information Seeking Strategies stage, and then actually get to the information in those sources. In the past, librarians and teachers spent a great deal of time on this part of the process. That's changing because they realize that Location & Access are only part of the overall process.

One important device that can save lots of time in Location & Access of resources is an index. Indexes of various kinds (yellow pages, directories in shopping malls, back-of-the-book indexes, online magazine databases) make it easier to find information. Indexes may not be exciting, but they really do save time and effort. Kids should always be on the lookout for indexes and they should know how to use them. Of course, indexes aren't the only way to locate and access information. Sometimes we just browse through the shelves, skim a book, or surf the Internet!

Parents can help their children with Location & Access in lots of ways. For example, they can help with math problems by searching the textbook or class notes with their children for similar problems and solutions. Or, they can demonstrate by example by using a back-of-the-book index while their children watch. One very practical way that parents can help is by driving or arranging for transportation for their children to the information source—a library, museum, or even a friend's house.

Use of Information

Locating and accessing information is easy compared to actually making use of the information found in the sources. This usually requires the child to: read, view, or listen; decide what's important for the particular task at hand; and finally extract the needed information. This isn't always easy to do, and could certainly take a considerable amount of time.

There's a lot parents can do to help in this stage. For example, a parent can "walk" a child through some tough reading to make sure the content is clear. A parent can also discuss various ways to skim or scan a reading. Then there are various information capturing methods a parent can help with. Showing students how to photocopy or how to highlight information will usually be a big help.

Synthesis

Synthesis involves organizing and presenting the information—putting it all together to finish the job. Sometimes Synthesis can be as simple as relaying a specific fact (as in answering a short-answer question) or making a decision (deciding on a topic for a report, a product to buy, an activity to join). At other times, Synthesis can be very complex and can involve the use of several sources, a variety of media or presentation formats, and the effective communication of abstract ideas.

Computer applications can help students organize and present information. Word processing, graphics programs, desktop publishing, databases, spreadsheets, and presentation packages can all help students put information together and present it effectively. Parents can help their children by arranging for access to a computer and software, especially word processing software. If there isn't a computer at home, parents can seek out other ways for their children to use one. Arranging for instruction in using a computer can be just as important as providing access to one.

Evaluation

In the Evaluation stage, children are asked to reflect on the process and result of their work. Are they pleased with what they have done? If they could do the project again, what might they do differently? Evaluation determines the effectiveness and efficiency of the information problem-solving process. Effectiveness is another way of saying, how good is the product? What grade are you likely to get? Efficiency refers to time and effort. If the children were to do the work again, how could they do as well, but save some time and effort?

It's important to get children to reflect on their performance. They need to think about their result and decide if they are pleased with it. It's not always necessary to get a top grade—sometimes OK is enough. At other times, they should want to strive for excellence. Kids need to understand and recognize the difference. They also need to think about the process. Where did they get stuck? Where did they waste time? All this so they can make changes next time. These kinds of self-reflection actions are true learning experiences. When students are self-aware, they evaluate themselves and can change their behavior for the better in the future.

Parents can help in Evaluation by encouraging their children to reflect in these ways. Parents can also help them to evaluate during the actual process when they get stuck. For example, if kids are having problems, parents can help them review what has already been done and help them think about what the end product will look like. Reconsider Task Definition and then talk about where the students are in the overall Big Six process.

The Big Six as Questions

We have also found that when acting as a guide, assistant, or coach, we can often work best with children by asking them questions related to the Big Six. The best and easiest way for us to use the Big Six to help students is to act as guides or coaches by "walking them through" the assignment and asking key Big Six questions along the way.

Figure 1 presents the Big Six in question form.

These questions can help guide students through any type of assignment—simple homework questions or problems, a report or project, a paper, or even a quiz or test. The questions focus attention on the specific task and the information needed to complete the task.

It's important to remember that the purpose of these questions is to guide and focus children, not to put them on the spot. It's fine to change the exact wording of the questions to match your own style or match the comprehension level of your children. It may also be useful to give an example by offering your own response to a question and then asking the children if they agree and can add another example.

It's not always necessary to go through all the questions and steps in order or in detail. We always check to make sure the children understand the task completely, since Task Definition is often the biggest problem. Sometimes it's good to jump directly to Synthesis at this point. Ask how they plan to organize and present their result. You can then come back to determining an Information Seeking Strategy, and work through Location & Access and Use of Information.

The amount of time and effort you spend on Information Seeking Strategies and Location & Access depends upon the nature of the assignment and the student's expertise. For a simple homework assignment, a student might just need one solid information source—generally class notes or a textbook. We want students to figure out the best (and easiest to use) source—the one that gives them the most accurate and complete information. Figuring this out shouldn't have to take a lot of time. More effort

---

Figure 1:

The Big Six Skills and Assignments—Key Questions

(1) Task Definition: determine what needs to be done and what information is needed.

Ask the student: • What do you need to do and what should it look like when you are done?
• What information do you need to do it?

(2) Information Seeking Strategies: figure out the resources to use.

Ask the student: • What resources can you use to get the job done?
• Which ones are the best to use for this job?

(3) Location & Access: get the resources and find the information in them.

Ask the student: • Where can you find these resources?
• Where is the information in the resources?

(4) Use of Information: read/hear/view the information and take out what's needed.

Ask the student: • Do you understand the information in the resources?
• Can you pull out what you need to do the assignment?

(5) Synthesis: put it all together.

Ask the student: • How does all this stuff fit together to complete the assignment?
• Does it look right?

(6) Evaluation: reflecting back on the result and the process.

Ask the student: • Have you done everything you were supposed to do?
• Do you feel OK about this work?
• If you had to do it again, what would you do differently?

---

should be spent on these steps if the assignment is a report or project, or if the children seem to have problems in selecting good sources.

More About the Big Six

When we talk about the Big Six, we are really referring to a process and an approach. The process encompasses the six stages from Task Definition to Evaluation. But the Big Six is also an approach—an approach to helping kids by using the Big Six process. Learning more about the Big Six as a process and as an approach should make it easier and more useful for you and your children:

(1) The Big Six process can be applied in all subjects and across all grade levels.

We have worked with students and teachers in all subject areas and in all grade levels. Students must complete assignments and solve problems in every class, in every subject, and in every grade. Each time, to be successful, the students need to figure out what they must do, and then gather and work with some information to finally produce something (even if it's a short answer on a quiz), and make sure it's OK before turning it in. That's what the Big Six is all about.

The Big Six is also applicable to everyday information problems, needs, and situations (for example, deciding what TV show to watch, deciding what to buy someone for a birthday present, or deciding how to earn extra money). Try talking through a typical decision-making situation with your children using the Big Six. It can be fun, and it will help them learn the process.

(2) The Big Six approach works with students of all ages.

As we discussed earlier, we generally simplify the Big Six into the Super Three when working with very young children. However, whether they realize it or not, younger students still go through the various stages of the Big Six when completing a task or an assignment.

For example, when kindergarten students are asked to make a picture of "signs of spring," they must first decide what it means to make a picture. Then they have to gather some information about spring and then they have to use that information to make a picture. Parents can use the Big Six process to help their children do a better job by doing one or more of the following:

- helping them to recognize that there are different ways to make a picture and asking them to explain what a really good picture would look like.

- brainstorming all possible places for information about spring and then helping to select the best place.

- helping them to locate and access the information.

- using the information resources, for example, walking outdoors and looking around, reading or looking through books, watching a video, or even just thinking hard themselves about signs of spring.

- again talking about what the picture might look like before starting to create.

- asking at the end if they are pleased with what they have done.

As students get older, the reflecting and questioning at each stage may get more complex, but the overall process is the same.

(3) While presented in a step-by-step fashion, the Big Six is not always linear.

People have different styles for completing tasks and solving problems. Some people are very systematic and like to go in order: 1-2-3. Others are less systematic. They prefer to follow their instincts. The Big Six does not assume or require that people go through the process in a fixed, linear way. If a student prefers to just start writing or to grab a resource and begin reading when given an assignment, that's fine.

Successful completion of assignments, however, does require completing each of the Big Six steps at some point in time. Students may not always be aware that they are working on a step—defining the task, using information, evaluating the result—but if they are successful, they are doing so.

(4) The Big Six process is necessary for solving problems and completing tasks.

Each of the Big Six steps is necessary for success in completing assignments. Some may refer to these steps in different terms, but successful information problem-solving is a process that includes each of the Big Six steps. Again, you may not always be aware that you have done a step—lots of us brainstorm possible sources quickly, and select what we consider to be the best without really thinking about it carefully—but we are still completing that step. Therefore, one way we can help kids is to ask them to reflect on the various steps in the process, so we can see where they might be having difficulty.

Another way to look at this is to work back from unsuccessful situations—not doing well on a paper or failing a test. If children do not do well, have them think about where they might have gone astray in terms of the Big Six. Did they fully understand the task? Did they gather the information needed? Were they able to understand the information resource and pull out needed information? Were they able to express themselves in a clear and meaningful way?

(5) The Big Six is not just for kids.

Everyone goes through the same general process (but often not in the same order) when solving problems or completing tasks. Elementary school students are confronted with information problems every day as are secondary school students and college students. Adults also are confronted with information problems in their work situations and in their personal lives.

Exactly how these problems are resolved depends upon the tasks themselves and one's own degree of sophistication, but in almost all cases, the steps taken to solve these problems are very close to the Big Six approach. The bottom line is that the Big Six Skills are useful whenever someone has an information problem or a decision to make based on information. And that's most situations!

Parents Using the Big Six Skills to Help a Student : An Example

The Big Six provides parents with a practical framework for helping their children. We will explain this in more detail with further examples in later chapters. Here, we offer a specific example of how a parent can use the Big Six to guide and assist a student.

Students are often asked to complete short answer questions at the end of a chapter in a text book, or to fill in a handout. Teachers make these kinds of assignments to ensure that the reading assignments are done.

▼

Sample Assignment: Science Vocabulary Words

Sue is a sixth grader who has a science vocabulary homework assignment. Her task is to define in her own words the 12 vocabulary words from the back of the chapter on the subject of volcanoes. All homework must be done in ink.

Parents' Role: Some Ways Parents Might Help

BEFORE

Task Definition:
- Ask Sue to explain briefly what she has to hand in for science.
- If she doesn't know what the assignment requires, ask to see the assignment and then help her define the task.
- If she doesn't have the assignment, ask her to think of other ways she can get it (for example, by calling a friend to find out what the assignment is).

Information Seeking Strategies:
- Talk about options that may be found in the textbook—the chapter, glossary, words highlighted.
- Discuss sources that might be used other than the textbook.

Location & Access:
- Explain to Sue, or remind her, that the words are probably in the index in the back of the book, and she should look for page numbers that are in the assigned chapter.

Evaluation:
- Together, try to estimate how much time this assignment might take.

DURING

Location & Access:
- Be available to help out with locating the terms.

Use of Information:
- Help Sue to understand what is written in the chapter and glossary.

Synthesis:
- If Sue is having trouble writing down the definitions, have her say them to you out loud first or perhaps use a tape recorder.

AFTER

Evaluation:
- Check to see if all 12 words are defined.
- Ask Sue if she wants you to check for grammar and punctuation.

This is just one example of how a parent might use the Big Six to guide a student through an assignment. We will offer many more specific examples in the chapters that follow. In general, parents help students by guiding them to:
- examine the task
- trouble-shoot when problems arise
- brainstorm alternatives
- reflect on the finished product.

The Result: Student Learning and Success

From a student's perspective, doing well in school work means getting the work done "right," and on time. Teachers call this effectiveness and efficiency. Doing assignments right means doing it effectively, completely, accurately, and according to the way the teacher will grade it. Doing well on assignments is also an issue of efficiency. Efficiency speaks to the time and effort required to complete the assignment. Students should be able to complete their work with a reasonable amount of effort and within a reasonable amount of time (relative to grade level and subject area).

One very direct and practical way to help students improve their effectiveness and efficiency in completing their homework and other assignments is to have them think about the assignments from a Big Six (information problem-solving) perspective. This means:

(1) recognizing that an assignment is just another information problem—similar to the personal and school problems they solve every day (e.g., deciding what to wear in the morning, answering questions in class, completing a major project, taking a test, selecting something to purchase from a store)

(2) being able to apply a process to solve these information problems

(3) learning specific information skills that are part of the process

(4) seeking assistance from teachers, library media specialists, and parents and family when necessary.

These suggestions and examples are just a beginning. The Big Six approach to homework and assignments offers parents a way to be partners with their kids in school success. The goal is to create a win-win situation in which students see their parents as helpful, and themselves as successful. There should be a concerted effort to try to avoid having the student become frustrated. To this end, parents need to take a familiar and consistent approach—one that lets students know what kind of help and guidance they can expect from their parents. Using the Big Six in the ways noted, our earlier scenario might now turn out differently:

Laura and her father are working on math problems. He sees she is having dif-
ficulty with long division and asks where they might find an example of how to
do similar problems. They brainstorm resources: the textbook, her notes, her
friend, the teacher. With a little coaxing, Laura decides that her notes might be
the best place to check. Laura gets out her notes
and together they locate a long division problem.
Her father asks if it is similar to the one she is
having difficulty with. She nods, and they
review the steps taken in the example.
Then they return to the troublesome
question, constantly referring back to
the notes. Afterwards, her father
asks, "Is it right? How do you
know?" Laura answers, "It's
just like the one we did in class."

Summary

In this chapter, we presented an overview of the Big Six approach and explained how parents can use the Big Six to help their children learn. Let's
summarize the key points:

(1) The Big Six is a process with a beginning, a middle, and an end.

(2) The Big Six Skills are: Task Definition, Information Seeking
Strategies, Location & Access, Use of Information, Synthesis, and
Evaluation.

(3) While the Big Six is presented as a step-by-step process, people
often jump around or loop back in the process. The important
thing is to complete each of the Big Six steps successfully at some
point in time.

(4) Guiding students may involve working with them to examine the task, trouble-shooting when problems arise, brainstorming alternatives, or reflecting on the finished product. The most common action is to ask the right questions.

(5) Success in homework and assignments means doing reasonably well in a reasonable amount of time and with a reasonable amount of effort.

(6) Using this approach, parents and their children can work together in a win-win situation.

2

What Your Children Face Every Day in School

Assignments

If we are to truly help our children with schoolwork, we must first understand exactly what they are being asked to do. What kinds of tasks and assignments do our children face every day? That's what we will focus on in this chapter, and we will give you some examples of how you can help your children.

Information in Schools

Schooling is essentially an information-oriented activity. All day long, students are bombarded with data and information—facts, statistics, concepts, opinions, directions, and tasks. Their job as a student is to sort through all this information and somehow "make sense" of it all.

There's a flow to this process of "making sense." Students start with simple facts and understandings. As they combine different pieces of information, they form broader understandings. This can be considered "knowledge." Finally, students do things based on knowledge. That's "action." That's what we want students to be able to do—turn raw data and information into knowledge and then take action based on that knowledge.

Unfortunately, in school, it's not always that simple or straightforward. Students face many different types of information tasks and problems. There are exercises, homework, projects, tests, and papers. These assignments take place in all subject areas. The data and information for addressing these various tasks and subjects come from many different sources: textbooks, non-fiction books, reference materials, videos, audio tapes, computer databases, and more.

The organization of the school day doesn't make this any easier. In a typical American school, at the sound of a bell, or at the tick of a clock, students must switch gears and stop learning math processes and start working with social studies concepts. Another tick, and the art project is put away and science homework is taken out. After lunch, it's time to take an English test.

While we might disagree with many aspects of the current educational system, our purpose here is not to criticize or advocate change. That won't provide immediate help to our kids right now. Instead, we will focus on ways to help students succeed regardless of the system.

It can be a chore for many kids to keep track of assignments, and all the information they will need to accomplish the various tasks. The teachers have explained the requirements—often more than once. But, for various reasons (for example, they got confused, their mind wandered, they were too embarrassed to ask when they didn't understand something), the students just didn't get it. And if they didn't understand what was asked of them in the first place, it will be very hard for them to do well.

For example, not too long ago, we visited an eighth grade social studies class in an urban middle school. We spoke to the students about the importance of task definition—the importance of really knowing what was expected in order to succeed. We asked, "tell us, what are you working on now?" It was a Friday, and they answered, "we have a test on Monday." "Fine," we said. "Now, tell us about the test. Is it going to be a big test or a small quiz?"

To our surprise, one-half of the class said it was going to be a big test, while the other half said it would be just a small quiz. After confirming with the teacher that it would be a chapter test, we probed further, "OK, will this be a comprehensive test covering material before the current chapter, or will it just cover the current chapter?" Again, there was disagreement in the class. Half the class said it would be comprehensive, while the rest were sure that it would just cover the current chapter. After checking with the teacher, we found that it would only cover the current chapter.

"One more question. Tell us about the test. Will it be a short-answer test or a multiple choice test, or will it be an essay test?" For the third time, the students disagreed with each other. Some expected a short-answer test, while others were sure it would be essays. The teacher explained that the test would be mostly short answers with one essay.

We then asked the teacher not to watch while we asked the students, "how many of you really intend to study for this test this weekend?" About three-quarters of the class raised their hands. "But," we stated, "if we hadn't asked you these questions, it's clear that some of you would be wasting a lot of time studying the wrong material and expecting to answer in the wrong way. We know that your teacher talked to you about the test, but for various reasons you hadn't all heard or understood. Your teacher isn't taking this test. It's you who will be affected if you do poorly on the test. That's why you must be the one to assume responsibility for knowing what's expected and in what form it is to be presented. That's what task definition is all about. If you don't know what's expected, ask or find another way to find out. If you want to do well, and want to do so without wasting a lot of time and effort, you need to make sure you understand what's really expected and how it should look when you are done. You need to do this for every assignment and every test in every subject. "

Parents can help students assume control and responsibility for their own learning by helping them work on task definition as the first part of the Big Six process. We can help students succeed if we can encourage them to:

(1) recognize the importance of fully understanding the task
(2) take on the responsibility of fully defining the task
(3) learn the right questions to ask.

As parents, you can help by modeling Task Definition yourselves. When you make a grocery list or write a memo for work, explain to your children how you are going about defining the task you will be involved with. Share your thoughts with them, and if feasible, include them in figuring out the exact nature of the problem and the types of information you will need to solve it.

Consider the "grocery list" task, for example. When getting ready to take your child with you to the market to buy groceries, discuss the tasks involved with your child (Task Definition). You might begin by explaining that you are going to need to make sure to buy enough food and supplies to last an entire week. You can then ask your child what other things are important to keep in mind as you prepare to go shopping. Children may think of ideas such as, "buy food that everyone likes," or "buy food that's healthy," or "save money (get good buys)." They are likely to surprise you and mention things you may not have thought about.

After discussing the task of grocery shopping with your children, ask them to think about the types of information they will need to know in order to make a shopping list. For example, they will need to know recipe ingredients in order to buy what's needed to make a particular dish. They might also want to know the nutritional contents of various foods, the likes and dislikes of family members, and the prices the stores are charging for various items. Again, open the discussion to see if your children can think of other things.

Once task definition is completed, you and your children can move on to the rest of the Big Six Skills. For Information Seeking Strategies, discuss possible information sources you can go to for needed information: cookbooks, family members, flyers from the supermarket, newspaper ads and television. Location & Access might involve using an index in a cookbook, talking with family, or finding newspaper ads. Use of Information might involve cutting out coupons, listing ingredients from a cookbook, or making a list of all the foods for each planned meal. Compiling the final shop-ping list is the Synthesis part of the Big Six process and you might even discuss different ways to organize the information on the list. Finally, you can reflect on the entire process with your children. Did you do a good job compiling the grocery list? How might you save time and effort next time?

But, we are getting a bit ahead of ourselves. If we, as parents, are to help our children with Task Definition, we must first review the nature of the tasks—the assignments. Then we can turn to ways of providing help.

Assignments

Assignments are integral parts of teaching and learning. Assignments are used as a teaching/learning method, and also as a means of determining whether learning has occurred. Students are evaluated by how well they perform on various assignments. In fact, teachers, schools, and the entire education system are judged on student performance.

Included among the more common assignments are:
  • homework assignments
  • class exercises (individual or group exercises)
  • exams (tests, quizzes)
  • essays, compositions
  • reports, research papers
  • classroom presentations
  • physical projects or multimedia projects.

The kinds of assignments that students receive can be broken down by format: written, visual, oral, or combination. Here we list typical examples in each of these categories.

Oral:

participate in a debate
interview a person
present an oral report
present a puppet show
sing a song
give a speech

Visual:

draw a cartoon
prepare a chart/graph
design a collage
make a diorama
prepare a drawing/painting
make a model
design a photo essay

Written:

design a booklet/pamphlet
write a character sketch
write a diary entry
write a letter
prepare a bibliography
write a newspaper article
write a poem or story

Combination:

invent and play a game
organize and present an interactive video
observe and record an experiment
design and show a computer-based multimedia program

Sometimes, students will be allowed to choose the format for an assignment. In this situation, parents can help by brainstorming with their children all the possibilities, and then by helping them weigh the options in terms of personal interest of the student, time and effort required, novelty, and how well a particular format will meet the given task.

Alternative Assessment

Teachers use a variety of methods to evaluate how well their students understand and are able to use lesson content. Traditionally these evaluations have related to the types of assignments described above as well as to paper and pencil quizzes and tests.

More recently, teachers are beginning to use "alternative" or "performance-based" assessment to evaluate students' work. Their intent is to assess students in more realistic situations. Traditional tests and assignments are considered artificial. They may not truly assess students' knowledge and abilities, or allow for differences in learning and performance styles. In fact, traditional forms of assessment tend to favor students who are particularly skilled at performing in traditional test situations.

Alternative assessment techniques attempt to evaluate students' knowledge and abilities in a range of settings over time. They often require students to demonstrate their competence by requiring them to create a product or project using content and concepts learned in the classroom. Some examples of alternative assessments include:

- portfolios of student work
- learning logs where students reflect on their activities and progress
- observation of students engaged in tasks and experiments
- authentic assessment, that is, observation of students in "real settings."

Ask your children and their teachers about the forms of assessment used in their school. If you don't recognize the format, find out more about it so you can help your children understand exactly what is expected of them, and on what basis their work will be evaluated. This is an important part of the Task Definition stage of the Big Six. Students often do not succeed because they don't really understand what is required of them or the criteria upon which their work is being evaluated.

Alternative assessments are well intentioned and generally do offer students a range of ways to show what they really know. However, alternative assessments can also be confusing because they are new and different. Parents can really assist here by helping their children understand what the assessment is trying to do, what the results of the assignments should look like, and how the final project will be graded.

Why Assignments?

Parents should understand the purpose behind an assignment and know how important the assignment is. For example, the purpose of an assignment may be to determine students' prior knowledge before instruction, or it may be an attempt to assess students' knowledge after instruction. The level of parent involvement will differ depending upon the purpose of the assignment.

Assignments are not given for grading reasons alone. Assignments can encourage students to learn new content and skills, review material already taught, remediate aspects of lessons that are not well understood, and extend knowledge or abilities beyond what's already learned. Here are some additional uses of assignments:

• to have students practice skills presented in the classroom and reinforce a lesson

- to prepare students for upcoming lessons to introduce new concepts or skills

- to determine individual student or group needs

- to assess students' mastery of content, processes, or skills

- to assess the degree of understanding students have of a topic or degree of skill achieved

- to evaluate which activities or topics need to be expanded

- to provide opportunities for students to use skills and concepts creatively to produce products/projects

- to promote higher order thinking by requiring students to use a skill or content knowledge in a new situation

- to summarize an activity or unit of study

- to evaluate which students need extra help or to provide an opportunity for students to complete work for which there was not enough time during the class or instructional period

- to have students learn how to evaluate their own work.

Summary

In this chapter, we focused on the tasks and assignments that students face in school every day. We also offered some examples of how you can help your children succeed in these assignments. Let's review the key points:

(1) Teachers assign homework and give quizzes and tests on a regular basis.

(2) Homework assignments, projects, and assessments such as tests and quizzes are used by teachers to provide students with opportunities to: practice skills, extend concepts taught in class, use information creatively, assess students' mastery, and prepare students for upcoming lessons.

(3) Doing well on homework, quizzes, and tests is important in the process of schooling. Parents should not only encourage their children to complete their homework, but also be able to help them be successful.

(4) Parents can use the Big Six Skills to help with any problem that students are having with homework assignments, quizzes or test questions.

In the next chapter, we will provide more detail about applying the Big Six Skills approach to assignments. We will explain how parents can be involved successfully in helping with all types of assignments.

3

The Big Six Applied

A Framework for Helping Children With Homework

In chapter two, we encouraged students and parents to consider all assignments including tests, reports, projects, and homework as information problems. In this chapter, we will explore the connection of assignment-to-Big Six Skills in more detail using homework examples. Homework is the most common form of school assignment, and parents can help students do well on their homework and save time and effort in the process.

Assignments as Information Problems: From a Big Six Perspective

Once students and parents have an understanding of the topic or content of an assignment, they need to have a strategy to get the work done. The Big Six process provides this strategy and parents can use it to help their children succeed.

We believe that students often have more knowledge than they were able to show on a homework assignment, a test, or through a project because:

- they didn't understand the instructions and what they were required to do
- they jumped right in without analyzing the task
- they didn't understand the questions because of the way they were worded
- they didn't really know what it takes to earn an "A."

If we can approach assignments with the Big Six in mind, we can help avoid these difficulties. Parents can help students to:

(1) focus on the problem (Task Definition)

(2) consider the information needed (Information Seeking Strategies)

(3) locate the needed information (Location & Access)

(4) recognize valuable information (Use of Information)

(5) organize and present logically (Synthesis)

(6) evaluate their own success (Evaluation).

From experience, we know that the first and last steps are crucial. If students don't understand a task fully, there is little chance they can complete it fully. Throughout this book we offer parents strategies they can use with their children to help them understand the assignments they are given.

Students should also be able to assess or evaluate their own work. Research shows "a student's perception of his/her capability to perform a task is one of the best predictors of school achievement" (Dempster, 1992). One of the foundations of the Big Six approach to assignments is that students need to be able to evaluate their own work, and determine effective ways to improve it.

The Big Six Applied: Using the Big Six to Help With Homework

The "Big Six Homework Consultation" we present below is something parents can use immediately to help their children. The Homework Consultation offers a number of different strategies parents can use to help their children with homework in meaningful ways. We focus here on homework because homework is the most common form of assignment— one which enters the home every day.

There are three stages where parents can help children with homework:

- before they begin—by helping students to prepare and organize

- during homework—by helping to trouble-shoot while students are working on the homework

- after they finish (but before they turn it in)—by helping to check and reflect.

Parents can use the Big Six Skills approach at each of these three stages to promote student success.

The Big Six Homework Consultation

(1) Preparing - Before

Parents can help students preview what the assignment requires and help them organize information.

Questions parents can ask, and help students answer, before they begin their homework include:

- What do you need to do?
- What information do you need?
- What should the assignment look like when you're done?
- How will you know if you've done a good job?

Very often, students have problems understanding what they are asked to do. This relates directly to Task Definition. The questions above help students focus on Task Definition and Evaluation. By asking those questions, parents can help students preview what the assignment requires before they begin. This will allow the students to think about what it will take to be successful and get a good grade.

(2) Trouble-shooting - During

Parents can help students identify the problems they are having with the assignment and suggest alternative solutions.

While students are doing their homework, parents can ask, and help students answer, the following questions:

- Are you finding the information that you need?
- Do you understand the information found in the resource?
- Are you able to pull out the important information that you need easily?
- Do you know how to organize the information to put the pieces together?

These questions help children focus on Information Seeking Strategies, Location & Access, Use of Information, and Synthesis. Here, parents can help by uncovering any problems their children are having, seeing if they are stuck, and if so, suggesting alternative strategies.

If the students seem to be really stuck, consider returning to Task Definition. Have the students state what they are trying to do. Is the task clear and does it seem doable?

(3) Checking - After

Parents can help students evaluate the quality of their homework to see if it was completed correctly. Parents can also help their children develop high standards for the homework and assignments they submit for grades.

Important questions parents can ask, and help students answer, after students have finished their homework include:

- Does your answer look right? Does it look the way the teacher expects it?
- Is this what you were supposed to do?
- Are you pleased with the result?
- Could you have done this better or quicker?

These questions help students focus on Evaluation. Here, the parents are helping their children to check and reflect. Students should be encouraged to evaluate the quality of their homework to see if the assignment was completed correctly.

Examples of the Big Six Applied to Homework

Sample Homework Assignment: Colonial Map

> *Don's fourth grade class is learning about Colonial America. His home-work assignment is to complete a map for social studies. Don's teacher has given him an outline map of the 13 original colonies. He is required to fill in the name of each colony. Don may use his textbook or any other source he may have at home.*

Parents' Role: Some Ways Parents Might Help

`BEFORE`

Task Definition:
- Ask Don to explain briefly what he has to do to complete his map assignment. If he doesn't know, ask him to show you the assignment.
- Ask Don what the most important part of the assignment is? Is it creating a nice looking map, or is it labeling the colonies correctly (or both)?
- Gently focus on any misunderstanding that Don might have about the assignment.

Information Seeking Strategies:
- Ask Don what source he intends to use. If he did not bring his text book home, discuss alternative sources.

Location & Access:
- Check to see if Don knows how to find the right map in his social studies book (or in another source).

DURING

Location & Access:

- Be available to help Don locate the colonies on his outline map and in the source he is using.

Use of Information:

- Encourage Don to look at the map in his textbook carefully before starting to put the names on his outline map.

Synthesis:

- Remind Don that sometimes neatness counts even though it was not mentioned in the assignment.

AFTER

Evaluation:

- Ask whether spelling and capitalization is important, and ask if he's checked?
- Offer to check over the map if he wants you to.
- Ask Don if the completed homework is the way the teacher wanted it, and is it ready to be turned in.

Sample Homework Assignment: One-page biography

Jilene is a seventh grader. Her physical education teacher gave the class a written assignment to complete. Jilene has to write a one-page biography about an athlete. She is supposed to choose a sports figure that she is interested in, but only knows a little about.

▼

Parents' Role: Some Ways Parents Might Help

BEFORE

Task Definition:

- Discuss how much information is needed in order to write the one-page biography.
- Confirm that the teacher expects Jilene to use more than one source—at least two in addition to the encyclopedia.

Information Seeking Strategies:

- Help Jilene figure out the best sources—those that have the best information and that are also easy to get to and use.

Synthesis:

- Encourage Jilene to include specific information in her essay and to cite her sources in the text.

DURING

Use of Information:

- Since Jilene sometimes has problems with taking notes on what's important, ask her to tell you about the sports figure verbally after she has read a source or section.
- Use an audio cassette or mini-cassette recorder to tape Jilene's comments, and then show her how she can take notes from her own comments.

Synthesis:

- Show Jilene how to make a simple chart to organize her information.

Evaluation:

- Encourage Jilene to be ready to turn in the assignment on time.

AFTER

Evaluation:

- Ask Jilene if it was easier to use the cassette recorder for note taking.
- Ask her how/if she might do the assignment differently next time.

Big Six Assignment Organizer

Barbara Jansen, a library media specialist in Texas, has worked with students, teachers, and parents on helping students with homework. Barbara has found that an assignment organizer is very useful in guiding students through homework using the Big Six process. Barbara has given us permission to reproduce her organizer, and we encourage you to make copies for use with your own children (see Appendix A).

Summary

- Parents can use the Big Six Skills approach to help their children with any problems the children are having with projects, reports, papers, homework, or even quizzes and tests.
- The Big Six Skills approach provides parents with a framework for approaching homework and other assignments.
- Parents can "walk" their kids through the process to prepare them for the assignment, trouble-shoot problems, or as a check back.
- Parents who use the Big Six Skills approach act as guides and helpers.
- When parents ask key questions based on the Big Six, they give students a model to use when students talk with their teachers about homework and assignments.

Computers, the Internet and Other Technologies

Can They Really Make a Difference?

Technology - What's all the Fuss?

"You don't have a computer at home? Isn't it about time? And, if you already have one, don't you need to consider upgrading to the latest model? You don't have Internet access? Come on. Get with it. After all, you do want to help your kids do better in school, don't you? You don't want to be left behind on the information superhighway, right?"

Parents everywhere are under great pressure to acquire a computer for the home or to upgrade the hardware and software for an existing home computer. One study by EPIC-MRA, based in Lansing, Michigan, reports that nearly one half of all American households own a computer, and 17% of those who do not already own one plan to buy a computer in 1996 ("Survey shows . . ." *Educational Technology News*, 1995). The hype and the promise of modern technology is enormous. We are surrounded by computers at work, while shopping, and even at play. It follows that there

should be one at home, right? In fact, the number one justification for the purchase of a home computer is educational use. Of course, the real number one use of computers at home is entertainment. Hmm, that seems like a lot of money for a toy.

We are now hearing the same kind of hype for the Internet—the so-called information superhighway:

> *"You don't have home access to the Internet? Come on. Get with it. After all, you do want to help your kids do better in school, don't you? Getting connected isn't a problem. All you need is to buy a modem, software, subscribe to a monthly service, and learn a whole bunch of commands. It's easy! And then your kids will have access to all the information in the world!"*

And that's part of the problem. Do your kids really need access to all the information in the world? Will this help them do better in school? In the last chapter, we explained how students must go through a full range of steps to solve an information problem. Locating and accessing information is just one of the Big Six Skills, and often it's not nearly as difficult as figuring out what exactly they are to do in the first place (Task Definition), deciding which resources might be the best to use (Information Seeking Strategies), and putting all the information together to solve the problem (Synthesis).

Now please don't get the wrong idea. We are very pro-technology. We do believe that technology can make a positive difference for kids. We have substantial first-hand experience helping students use computers and the Internet to improve their work. Computers can be personal productivity boosters. They expand our ability to accomplish certain tasks. But too often, computers and other technologies are presented as solutions in search of problems, or as answers without questions. It's like the cartoon below:

Technology is the answer, now what was the question?

We believe the important question is, how can our kids improve their school work? How can they do better on:

- defining the problem
- determining an information seeking strategy
- locating and accessing the information
- using the information found
- putting it all together in a finished product
- evaluating their success.

Can technology help with this? Absolutely. We believe the key to using various technologies in meaningful ways is to consider the technologies as part of the information problem-solving process—that is, in relation to the Big Six. Various computer capabilities—including the Internet—can be very important for students' success in accomplishing each of the Big Six Skills. A very useful way to look at computers and related technologies is to consider them as valuable tools that can boost students' abilities in carrying out the Big Six.

Tools help us do a better job—be more effective. Tools also help us save time and effort—be more efficient. If we want to build a table, we might use a saw to cut up pieces of lumber. We might even use an electric saw because it helps us be more accurate, and certainly saves time and effort. We would use a range of other tools for other parts of the project, for example, a measuring tape to determine proper lengths, a screwdriver to fasten pieces together, a sander to smooth the wood, and a paint brush to apply a finish. Hopefully, these tools improve performance and save time and effort.

Similarly, if students need to write a report on the animals of Australia, they might decide to use a word processing program on a computer to organize and present their information. They also might use a range of other technologies, for example electronic mail to discuss the assignment with their teacher, an electronic database on animals as an information resource, and a graphics program to create visuals for the report. Hopefully these computer-based tools will improve performance and save time and effort.

We will focus the remainder of this chapter on a discussion of various technologies that can be used as tools in a Big Six context. First, we will explain some of the computer technologies that are available today, and those that are likely to be available tomorrow. We will also describe the capabilities of these technologies in terms of the Big Six—that is, how a particular technology can be applied to one or more of the Big Six Skills. We will then turn things around, and review the Big Six process with technologies in place. This will illustrate how we can use technology effectively and efficiently. Finally, we will return to the question posed at the beginning of this chapter—do we as parents need to provide computers at home, and if so, a computer with what capabilities?

Computer Technologies: Today and Tomorrow

We are not going to provide a complete introduction to computers and related technologies in this book. We will, however, offer you some general, overview information. If you are someone who doesn't know very much about computers, the Internet, or technology in general (these folks are sometimes called "newbies"), there are lots of books available that are simple and straightforward. Look for one that doesn't try to cover too much, seems understandable after skimming the first chapter, and was written this year. Technology changes so quickly that books, no matter how good, can become outdated quickly.

You might try to find someone patient who can help you along. Sometimes the best person to explain things to you is your own child or another young person. We have learned much of what we know about technology from our students, our children, and our friends' children.

Of course, you don't need to know or learn everything there is to know about computers in order to help your kids use computers effectively and efficiently. In fact, you really don't need to know how to use computers at all! As we've said before, your role is guide and helper, not teacher. As parents, we can first make sure that our children have access to computers—in school, through libraries and other public places, and if feasible, at home. We can also ask Big Six-type questions to get our kids thinking about how they might apply computers and technology to Big Six tasks.

When we speak about computer technology, we usually begin with hardware and software. Hardware refers to the actual computer equipment itself—the electronic circuits in some form of metal or plastic box, the screen, keyboard, mouse, printer, modem, etc. The hardware also includes various forms of computer memory. Memory is needed to store the software and the information that computers use to do their job. Memory comes in lots of different forms—electronic circuit boards called "chips" (often referred to as RAM—random access memory), floppy disks, hard disks, and CD-ROM. A typical computer may use all of these forms of memory. One of the major differences in price among various computers is the amount of memory that is available.

It soon becomes complicated to consider all the hardware options available for computers. And, it gets further complicated because the technology is constantly changing—mostly for the better. The technology is improving so rapidly that we seem to get more capabilities (usually defined as power and memory) for a given price as time progresses. *[Note: If you are thinking about purchasing a computer and don't really know very much about them, seek out assistance before buying. There are numerous decisions to make—some with important functional and price considerations.]*

Again, fortunately, you really don't need to know too much about hardware in order to think about how to use technology to assist your children. That's because the hardware itself doesn't really do anything without software. Software includes (1) sets of instructions (called programs) and (2) data and information that tells the computer what to do. Computers can't do anything without software. So, if we want to focus on using computers as tools, we need to focus on the software.

Computer Software from a Big Six Perspective

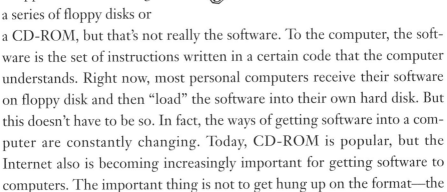

Software isn't really something you can touch. When you buy a particular piece of software, you'll likely get a shrink-wrapped box containing a series of floppy disks or a CD-ROM, but that's not really the software. To the computer, the software is the set of instructions written in a certain code that the computer understands. Right now, most personal computers receive their software on floppy disk and then "load" the software into their own hard disk. But this doesn't have to be so. In fact, the ways of getting software into a computer are constantly changing. Today, CD-ROM is popular, but the Internet also is becoming increasingly important for getting software to computers. The important thing is not to get hung up on the format—the floppy disk or CD-ROM or whatever, but to focus on the capabilities of the software. What it does is what really counts.

Sometimes software vendors will combine a number of software capabilities into one "package." Clarisworks™ and Microsoft Works™ for example, combine word processing, electronic spreadsheets, database management, and telecommunications. The functions are still the same as those described below. It's just that they all come together in one program.

Word Processing

Description: Word processing is the most widely used and popular type of computer software. Word processing helps you create all types of documents—reports, essays, letters. The best thing about word processing is that it makes it easy to make changes and revisions before you print out a final copy of your document. It's also easy to move around individual words, sentences, or even whole sections of a document. Word processing easily allows you to change the way a document looks, for example the margins, font type and size, and the style (underlining, bold, italics). Most people prefer word processing over tools such as a pen and paper or a typewriter because of word processing's flexible revising and formatting capabilities.

Today's word processing programs include a range of advanced features.

Word Processing:

Entering text	= organize/present	= Synthesis
Cut/paste, edit functions	= organizing	= Synthesis
Note taking, cut/paste	= extraction	= Use of Information
Spell/grammar/style check, Thesaurus	= judging the product/process	= Evaluation

The software can check the spelling, grammar, and even the writing style of a document—highlighting possible errors and suggesting alternatives. It's also possible to create tables, to add graphics, to use special symbols or scientific notation, or to highlight a section of text by shading or putting a box around it.

The Big Six Connection: Word processing is clearly a valuable tool. The revising and editing functions make it easier for students to organize their information and present a final version of their work. This is Synthesis. While the various formatting capabilities make a document look neater, the most important capabilities are those that allow for editing and moving information around.

Word processing can also increase a student's ability to take notes (the extraction part of Use of Information). One way is for students to type notes directly into a computer. This can save time and effort. However, we've also seen situations where it creates more problems! From experience, we've found that the best way to use a computer for note taking is to first develop a rough outline for the paper or project. The students should type the outline into the computer and label each section clearly. Then, they can type the notes under the relevant section—or move (cut and paste) notes from one section to another.

It's essential to keep track of the source of the various notes. Teachers (and librarians) insist on proper citing of sources, footnotes, and bibliographies. Good use of footnotes and a solid bibliography can often make the difference between a good paper (and grade) and an outstanding one. Word processing can help here too. First, keep track of all resources used in a separate bibliography section or separate document. Then, keep a quick reference to the resources with the notes—author-date-page in parenthesis like this example: (Eisenberg & Berkowitz, 1996, p. 33). Any directly quoted text should be placed in quotation marks. Later, students can paraphrase and delete the quotes, or decide to use the direct quote as is.

Word processing can also help when it's time to check over the final product before submitting it to the teacher. Spelling and grammar checking features work by highlighting a word or section of text that may need correcting. Generally, the user is offered some alternatives to choose from. The thesaurus function works the same way by suggesting some synonyms. But, your children must still make the decisions. They still decide on the proper spelling or use of words. For example, spelling software is usually good at catching typos, but often wrong on proper names. The students are still analyzing and selecting. All this interaction becomes a valuable learning experience. And, your children are involved in Evaluation—judging their product and even thinking about their own skills and abilities.

Related Software: Desktop Publishing

Desktop publishing is a type of computer software that takes word processing one step further. Desktop publishing programs such as PageMaker™ and Quark Express™ can be used to create professional-looking printed publications, for example, newsletters, books, brochures, and pamphlets. Desktop publishing makes it easy to combine text and graphics in unique ways. Desktop publishing is an important and widely-used tool for Synthesis. However, in schools, it's likely to be used only by students in the upper grades working on very special publications such as the school newspaper or yearbook.

Graphics Programs

Description: Graphics programs refer to the range of software products that help users create, edit, and manipulate still and moving images. They are the electronic versions of crayons, paints, and paper. They also help us do the electronic equivalent of cutting and pasting pictures from magazines. Graphics programs range from simple draw and paint programs (Kid Pix™, Superpaint™) to sophisticated photographic and video editors (Photoshop™, Adobe Illustrator™).

Graphics programs aren't meant to replace physical painting and drawing but they may help those of us who may not be talented in drawing or painting. They help us draw circles, ellipses and other shapes, add shading or color, change sizes, or move parts of pictures around. They also make it easy to edit, improve, or use only parts of our own work or other existing artwork. For example, there are numerous collections of computer-based images (called "clip art") available and these can be used in various ways to enhance a document.

Big Six Connection: We are all familiar with the old cliché, "a picture is worth a thousand words." But not everyone is able to communicate easily and effectively in pictures. That's what graphics programs do. They help students create, change, and organize pictures. Creating, editing, and organizing are skills associated with Synthesis —stage five of the Big Six.

Students adapt to these programs quickly and learn how to create various images and use them as products themselves, or use them in various projects and reports. Sometimes it's as basic as creating a chart, graph, or table for use in a report. At other times, the final project itself may be an illustration or series of pictures. In all of these cases, students are engaged primarily in Synthesis—creating, organizing, and presenting information.

Graphics programs can also help with the Use of Information—engaging and extracting relevant information. For example, students may look through a collection of clip art on a CD-ROM and choose a cartoon image to use in a report. Or, they may use a scanner (a piece of computer hardware) to put a print picture into electronic form. Then they might use a graphics program to select part of the picture and reduce the size so it fits into the space available in a paper. These are examples of how graphics programs can help students engage and extract information.

Some teachers are rightly concerned about the potential for plagiarism when students use graphics programs. That's why it is essential for students who use clip art or a scanned image to give proper credit to the source of the image. This holds true for word processing or cutting and pasting from print sources as well. In many cases, it is acceptable for students to use information and images created by others. Parents can help their children by emphasizing the necessity to cite full and complete sources—especially for images.

Teachers and library media specialists are also finding that some students copy too much directly from sources. This was a problem before computers as well, but current technology makes it extremely easy to copy and paste large sections or images from electronic reference works. Understanding what is OK and what's not OK in terms of directly using others' work is an important part of Use of Information. It is also not an easy skill to learn. Teachers and library media specialists are working hard to teach students when to quote directly and cite versus paraphrase and cite versus combining information from multiple sources and not citing. Parents may need to check with their children's teachers or look over a report or project to see if a problem exists.

Related Software: Graphics and media software are becoming increasingly popular. Today, there are software programs that help create and manipulate sound, video, and a range of multimedia. Even some of the high-end word processing programs include drawing, painting, and other graphics capabilities. Graphics tools are also important in the multimedia and presentation software programs we will describe in the next section.

All of these tools help students organize and present information—Synthesis. They sometimes help with use of information as well. Again, it's not necessary for parents to know how to use each type of program personally. Parents can help by recognizing the purpose of a particular software tool and helping the student realize the connection to the Big Six. A parent can also help students determine if they need a particular software tool to help them in a given situation.

Presentation Software and Multimedia Software

Description: This type of software expands on the Synthesis capabilities offered by word processing and graphics programs. Students of all ages can use presentation software to create multimedia shows, slides, overhead transparencies, or special handouts.

Once exclusively "high-end" and expensive, multimedia programs such as HyperStudio™ and Linkway™ offer students some impressive capabilities for combining text, graphics, sound, pictures, and video. Using this type of software, students can create and edit various forms of multimedia, and then combine them in various sequences. Powerpoint™, Persuasion™, and Macromind Director™ are examples of sophisticated presentation and multimedia programs.

Big Six Connection: Presentation software is specifically designed for creating, organizing, and presenting information—Synthesis activities. As with graphics and word processing, students can use presentation software to edit and revise their products relatively easily. These programs also greatly expand the variety of formats for student expression. Students who have a difficult time writing words may find it more effective to use multimedia to communicate what they know.

Related Software: Almost any computer program that involves Synthesis is related to multimedia and presentation software. For example, there are programs labeled as "authoring tools." These programs help teachers and others create presentations for particular situations. The Internet, which we describe in more detail below, also involves multimedia presentation and authoring. Then there are program packages that help people create multimedia documents called web pages (or home pages) that can be shared through the Internet. We will explain these in more detail later.

Electronic Spreadsheets and Database/File Management Programs

Description: Spreadsheets and database/file management software are essential information tools in work settings and have much to offer schools and the home. These programs allow users to store, organize, manipulate, and present all types of information. While both types of programs can handle various data formats, electronic spreadsheets do so primarily for numerical information (for example, budgets and finances, scientific data). The various database/file management programs handle mostly text (for example, names and addresses, product information, information about places or things).

Examples of spreadsheet programs are Lotus 1-2-3™ and Excel™. Dbase™, Rbase™, Filemaker™, and Microsoft Access™ are examples of database/file management programs. In addition, all of the "works" or combination products (e.g., Clarisworks™ and Microsoft Works™) include both spreadsheet and file management capabilities.

Big Six Connection: Spreadsheets are powerful tools for Synthesis—organizing and presenting all types of numerical information. They make it easy to enter numbers into a table, perform various mathematical functions on the numbers (from simple addition or subtraction to setting up complicated formulas) and to display or print the result as a table, chart, or graph. Spreadsheets are particularly useful in science and math classes and labs. Students can store, process, and present data from experiments in much the same way as scientists do. In math, spreadsheets are "supercalculators" and can be used to work through problems, carry out various statistical operations, and graph functions. Spreadsheets are also highly useful for creating graphs, tables, and charts for projects, reports, and other assignments in social studies, health, English, and most other subjects.

Database/file management programs are also powerful Synthesis tools applicable across subjects. These tools are particularly good at handling text information. Students can use these programs to create databases and printed tables that supplement printed reports or projects. These programs may also completely replace the reports themselves. As with spreadsheets, database/file management programs are applicable across subjects. We have seen impressive databases created in science, social studies, and health classes.

Related Software: Spreadsheets and database/file management programs are useful and popular because they help store, organize, retrieve, and report information. Individuals and businesses use these tools to cope with information overload.

Because many of us want to deal not only with text and numbers, but also with pictures, graphics, video, and sound, database software producers are developing programs that handle all forms of media and resources—video, audio, images, statistics, time and project management, words, numbers, plans. At various times, students may need to use advanced tools such as these.

Parents need not know all about products such as these in order to help their children. It's enough for them to realize that specialized tools for organization and presentation (Synthesis) exist. Parents can then discuss these options when their children are working through elaborate assignments.

Electronic Information Resources:
Online Reference Works, Databases, Indexes

Description: There is an "information explosion" in the number and range of electronic resources available in libraries, schools, and the home. All types of reference works are now available in electronic format including:

- encyclopedias
- atlases
- special subject resources
- guides and handbooks
- library catalogs (often called online public access catalogs—OPACS)
- magazine indexes and newspaper indexes
- magazines and newspapers in full-text.

There are a number of ways to gain access to these electronic resources. Most are available on CD-ROMs—thin, silver, circular disks that are very similar to music CDs. A computer must have a CD-ROM drive built-in or attached to use CD-ROMs. Various electronic resources are also stored on local computer systems in schools or public libraries. Some electronic resources come already loaded on the personal computer you buy for your home. Electronic resources are also available through the Internet and other computer networks (for example, America Online™ and Prodigy™).

If all this seems at bit overwhelming to you, you are not alone. People in all types of settings from businesses and government offices, to colleges and universities and elementary and secondary schools, are struggling with the problem of knowing which resources to use, knowing how to gain access to those resources, and knowing how to find needed information within the resources. One good way of dealing with this struggle is to use the Big Six approach.

Big Six Connection: Three of the Big Six Skills deal directly with electronic information resources: Information Seeking Strategies, Location & Access, and Use of Information.

Selecting from hundreds (soon to be thousands) of available electronic resources is not easy. From a Big Six perspective, we are talking about developing Information Seeking Strategies. Students should be able to consider the full range of resources (including electronic resources) available to them and then be able to select the best resource or resources for a given task. By "best" resources, we mean "most appropriate" not necessarily highest in quality. Quality is certainly a major concern, but it's not the only thing to consider. We need to also consider availability, cost, and ease-of-use. For example, the "best" resource about the political situation in the former Soviet Union may be a special report from a private "think tank." However, the report may be fairly complicated, expensive, and likely to be above all but the top students' reading abilities. More appropriate resources are electronic magazine and newspaper resources available in the school library media center.

We want students to be able to make these choices as part of their Information Seeking Strategies. They should be able to recognize the full range of possibilities and then be able to select the most appropriate resources based on quality, availability, currency, and ease-of-use. Students should not be restricted to what's available at home. Regular use of school library media centers and public libraries is an essential Information Seeking Strategy. Not only are there far more resources available in libraries than at home, but there are trained professionals there who can provide direction and assistance.

Using electronic information resources also requires Location & Access skills. Once an Information Seeking Strategy is determined, students must be able to get to the electronic resource and then be able to find the needed information within the resource. As resources and databases get

Related Software: The most important related software here are those electronic resources available through the Internet and other online services. We will discuss these in the next section.

The Internet

The interest in and popularity of the Internet has surprised even so-called computer experts. In this section, we will try to unravel some of the mystery and the hype about the Internet and we will focus on how children can use the Internet to boost their skills and succeed in school.

The Internet is currently the hottest thing in computing and communications. It seems that everyone is "connecting" by getting a modem (a hardware device that enables a computer to communicate through telephone lines), acquiring a communications software program, and signing up with an Internet service provider. Why are they doing so? Why connect to the Internet? For two reasons: (1) to communicate, and (2) to get information. When people talk about sending or receiving e-mail, they are referring to the communications part of the Internet. When they talk about surfing the World Wide Web, they mean using the information gathering capabilities of the Internet.

The Internet is an electronic network, similar to cable TV or the telephone network, that connects millions of computers around the world to each other. Some of the computers connected to the Internet are the fast and powerful computers of universities, libraries, government agencies, and businesses. These computers (sometimes called file servers) provide information and various information services to anyone connected to the Internet. These computers are usually directly wired to the Internet and are connected all the time.

Most people, however, connect to the Internet through their personal or desktop computers at work or at home. These millions of people use the Internet primarily for the two reasons stated above: (1) to communicate with each other, and (2) to gain information and information services from the larger computers and from each other.

While the Internet has much to offer students and parents, it's not, as some have predicted, a replacement for libraries and schools. We believe it's more useful to think of the Internet as a powerful communications and information utility that expands the capabilities and functions of libraries and schools. Through the Internet, individuals at home can connect to libraries and information sources throughout the world. This expands the role of libraries because putting people in touch with information is what libraries are all about. The Internet can make it possible for adults and children across the world (or across town) to participate in the same classes, seminars, and workshops. This expands the role of schools be-cause providing learning opportunities is what schools are all about.

One major concern people have about the Internet is that children may gain access to or stumble across inappropriate materials. Parents should realize that the Internet is a wide-open communications and information environment. It's like visiting a major metropolitan city. There are plenty of interesting and valuable things there (museums, libraries, historical places), but you wouldn't let young children wander around alone or with-out guidance. Even older children may need some direction or assistance. It's the same with the Internet. We want to help our children experience the best of the Internet and avoid the less desirable sections. Parents can do this by learning about the Internet themselves, by working with teach-ers, librarians and others in the schools, and most importantly, by talking to their children about appropriate use of the Internet, and about what to do if something seems strange.

In the remainder of this section, we will look at the Internet in more detail. Just as we focused on computers in terms of software capabilities and how they relate to the Big Six, we will similarly look at various Internet capabilities.

Electronic Mail (E-mail)

Description: You can use electronic mail (e-mail) to send and receive messages to and from another person or group of people. All this takes place on your computer screen, but the actual transmission of the message takes place through the Internet. E-mail is not "live" and immediate (like talking on the telephone). It's more like sending or receiving a letter, but the sending/receiving takes place in seconds or minutes rather than days.

Beyond the normal hardware and software required to connect to the Internet, using e-mail requires an e-mail account (or address) and an e-mail software program. In schools, the e-mail address is usually assigned by a teacher, library media specialist or someone running the computer system. In your home, it's assigned by the service providing your connection to the Internet. The school or Internet service provider will also supply the e-mail software program.

Many different e-mail programs are available. Some common e-mail programs are Eudora™ and Pine Mail™. Providers such as America Online™ and Compuserve™ offer their own e-mail programs. In addition to "send" and "receive" commands, most e-mail programs allow users to compose and edit messages, keep address books of frequently used names and addresses, and save, store and organize previous messages.

More and more schools are providing e-mail accounts to students and teachers so they can communicate with each other and with other students and teachers around the world. School e-mail accounts usually have limits in terms of connection time allowed and storage space for saving messages. The accounts may also expire at the end of the school year. School e-mail accounts are not guaranteed to be private and may be monitored. In fact, it's not a good idea to assume that any e-mail is secure and private.

Big Six Connection: Most of the software we described in the previous section focused on boosting the Big Six capabilities of Synthesis, Information Seeking Strategies, and Location & Access. E-mail provides assistance with the first, and often the most difficult Big Six step: Task Definition.

E-mail helps students communicate with teachers and with each other about assignments, tasks, or problems. During the school day, students and teachers are constantly on the run. There may be little time for communication regarding the specifics of a test or assignment. Students can use e-mail to leave messages for teachers in school or they might even do so from home, expecting a response within 24 hours. Conversely, teachers can leave messages for students, reminding them about important aspects of assignments or instructions for an exam. Students can also use e-mail to communicate with other students in their class, school, or anywhere in the world. They can seek advice or work together on joint projects.

Beyond Task Definition, students can use e-mail to ask others if information is available on a topic (Information Seeking Strategies) or where they might find the information (Location & Access). Students can also use e-mail to conduct an electronic interview (Use of Information) and gain needed information from someone on the Internet. Students can also interact with each other worldwide as "e-mail" or "keyboard" pals. They can learn about other cultures, practice writing and reading, and can send messages to each other about their work and studies.

Teachers can use e-mail to give feedback to students on their work (Evaluation). Students can submit a section or example from a paper or project, and teachers can send comments back via e-mail.

Related Software: In addition to person-to-person messaging, e-mail does support some group communication. For example, you can send the same e-mail message to more than one person at the same time. In fact, the address book function of many e-mail software programs includes some capability to create "lists" of people so that you can easily send the same message to an entire group. Teachers might use this capability to send a note to the entire class. Group e-mail is expanded even further in newsgroups and listservs which we will discuss in the next section.

Other Internet communications capabilities that can help with Task Definition and other Big Six steps include Internet Relay Chat, MOO, and other "chat" capabilities. These programs allow individuals and groups of people to interact "live" through the Internet, primarily through text—not sound or video. Once connected to the Internet, people can issue a command that allows them to connect to a chat room or MOO where other people are connected and available for conversation. As we noted earlier in our discussion of general Internet use, parents should be involved with their children in the use of chat and MOO to ensure these capabilities are used appropriately.

Graphics, video, and sound are capabilities that we are beginning to see incorporated into Internet communications projects. CUSeeMe, for example, allows video interaction through the Internet using relatively inexpensive cameras connected to computers. Video/sound e-mail and interactive conferencing are likely to be staple Internet functions within a few years.

Electronic Discussion Groups (listservs, newsgroups)

Description: When people discuss how useful the Internet is, they frequently talk about how the Internet brings people together. Listservs and newsgroups make it possible for people to communicate and work together. There are thousands of listservs and newsgroups on the Internet. They are electronic discussion groups organized around various topics of personal and professional interest. You can find out about specific listservs or newsgroups from books and directories about the Internet, magazine articles, and of course, by talking with other people.

Listservs are often referred to as electronic communities because in many listservs, people develop a strong sense of camaraderie. Listservs operate through e-mail. You subscribe to a listserv by sending an e-mail message to a designated address, and from that moment on you will receive every e-mail message that's sent to that listserv. You become part of a worldwide e-mail conversation (actually conversations because there may be many different topics being discussed at the same time) related to the topic of the listserv.

Newsgroups are also electronic discussion groups, but they operate differently. Newsgroups are more like bulletin boards. You subscribe to a newsgroup, but you don't see any of the messages unless you choose to do so. There's still a group discussion, but you don't see every message unless you choose to do so. Some say there's less of a feeling of community with newsgroups, but it's easier to manage all the message traffic.

Big Six Connection: Electronic discussion groups can contribute to many of the Big Six steps. Teachers can set up listservs just for their classes. Through the listservs, students and teachers can discuss assignments (Task Definition) or alternative information resources (Information Seeking

Strategies, Location & Access). The teacher may also post information re-lated to an assignment or test for students to read (Information Seeking Strategies).

Listservs and newsgroups contain massive amounts of information about various topics. One possible Information Seeking Strategy is to seek infor-mation through listservs or newsgroups. The students must then go through Location & Access to gain the desired information. However, in these instances the most crucial Big Six skill is Use of Information. Stu-dents must read the information carefully and then determine whether the information is applicable to their task and whether it's reliable. People are correct when they say there's lots of garbage on the Internet. Sifting through all the information and determining what is valuable is an essen-tial Big Six information skill.

Related Software: Many groups and listservs save previous messages in archives. These archives become rich resources of information, but searching through them can be difficult. Finding accurate, reliable, au-thoritative information within archives can tax the Location & Access skills of even the most sophisticated searchers. The live "chat" capabilities we discussed earlier expand the electronic discussion aspects of listservs and newsgroups.

World Wide Web (WWW)

Description: One of the reasons the Internet is receiving so much atten-tion is the World Wide Web. It's the "hottest" of the "hot." The World Wide Web (also called WWW or sometimes just Web) is the information side of the Internet. The Web is a massive, interrelated information net-work. It's composed of tens of thousands of interlinked information files stored on computers connected to the Internet. These files, called web sites or home pages, can contain text, graphics, video, and sound. Web sites exist on every topic imaginable. The Web is growing at an incredible rate: in 1996 there were estimates that the number of WWW sites was doubling every 50 days! Your biggest challenge is to sift your way through all the information and pages to find what you really want and need. When people talk about "surfing the Internet," they really mean looking through the vast stores of information on the World Wide Web.

Once connected to the Internet, you access the WWW through a software program called a "browser." A browser allows you to connect to any specific Web site and move from one Web site to another. Web pages are identified by a special address called a "URL"—uniform resource locator. You've probably seen these listed in newspapers or magazines or on television. They always start with: http://, for example: http://ericir.syr.edu (AskERIC site); http://cnn.com (CNN site); http://usatoday.com/ (*USA Today* site).

Browsers can help you use the WWW in various ways. They keep track of the sites you use regularly, and they allow you to print and save useful information. The most popular WWW browser is Netscape™, but there are others including Microsoft's Explorer™ and Lynx™. Lynx™ is a browser that provides text-only access to the WWW. It is used by people whose Internet service provider doesn't yet offer a graphic connection to the Internet.

Browsing is not really a very efficient way to seek information. It's okay for checking out the news, or for entertainment, but it doesn't help those looking for in-depth information on specific topics. Most WWW users, quickly tire of simply surfing from site to site. They want to search more directly for information. A number of software programs have been developed to meet this need. These "searchers" or "search engines" (e.g. Yahoo, Lycos, Infoseek) are tools designed for seeking out specific information on the WWW. Searchers are really the keys to being able to use the Web for specific information needs.

Until very recently it was a big deal to create and maintain a home page on the Internet. Now, it's relatively easy and getting easier. Many schools, teachers, and students are creating World Wide Web pages. The WWW is based on a standard code called HTML—hypertext markup language. Browsers, searchers, and other World Wide Web tools rely on this common code. Creating a Web page means learning how to put the right codes in the right places in a file. This can be done with a word processor, but now there are special HTML authoring tools that help you do this.

Big Six Connection: The World Wide Web is a massive information system. As students work through Information seeking strategies, we recommend they proceed with caution. The Web isn't a single information resource. It's really thousands of information resources. Web sites differ greatly in quality, reliability, depth-of-coverage, and organization. If students decide that surfing or even searching the Web is a reasonable Information Seeking Strategy for a particular task, they need to consider carefully what exactly they hope to gain, and how they will judge the quality and usefulness of a particular Web site.

The Web presents the greatest challenge of any information system in terms of Location & Access. This is due to the wide range in quality of sites, the present size of the Web, the explosive growth of the Web, and the difficulty of organizing Web information. The searcher programs are somewhat helpful, but regular WWW users will tell you that the search engines are quite limited. When you search, you rarely zero in on exactly what you are looking for. You will get many sites that are not relevant, or you may not find a specific match at all. That doesn't mean that the WWW doesn't contain what you are looking for. It just means that the search tools haven't found it.

Students need to learn how to interact with WWW information and extract useful information. These are Use of Information skills and involve such tasks as downloading files, saving files, e-mailing information from the WWW, and cut/paste.

More and more schools are providing opportunities for students to create their own WWW pages. These can be relatively simple examples of student work, or elaborate multimedia presentations related to assignments, extra-curricular activities, or personal interest. Creating a Web page is a major effort in Synthesis requiring new skills in organizing, combining, composing, creating, and presenting information. Most students are excited about and eager to learn these skills.

Related Software: The Internet is not the only computer information network. America Online™, Prodigy™, Compuserve™, The Microsoft Network™ and others provide e-mail, information resources, and other services. Still, the overwhelming popularity of the Internet caught many of those networks by surprise. To compensate, they all now provide access to the Internet as part of their services. In fact, many networks are scaling back their own unique information services in favor of trying to offer improved Internet access.

The World Wide Web is popular because it is graphical, colorful, and relatively easy to use. But the Web is not the only information system on the Internet. For example, "ftp" (file transfer protocol) is a software program that provides access to a massive system of files, documents, and software on the Internet. To find out what's available through ftp, there's another software program called "Archie." The drawback is that Archie and ftp are not very easy to use.

Another Internet information system is "Gopher" - a text-based system that organizes information through various menus. Gopher was the most popular information system on the Internet just a few years ago. It was relatively easy to use and worked even with limited text-based or slower connections to the Internet. But it isn't easy to create Gopher sites (there's no code like HTML), and Gopher lacks the graphics and flash of the WWW. But, while new Gopher development is minimal, and most Gopher sites are converting their materials to the Web, there are still many valuable resources available only through Gopher.

As you can probably tell, the Internet is not a fixed, static system. New developments appear continually in the information available on the Internet and in the tools available to use that information. As we help our children use the current Internet, we need to also help them expect and be ready for new options.

┌─ Figure 3: ──────────────────────────────────────

REVIEW CHART:
Internet Capabilities and the Big Six

E-mail	= Task Definition
	Evaluation
WWW/browsers (Netscape, Explorer, Lynx)	= Information Seeking Strategies Location & Access
WWW/searchers (Lycos, Yahoo, Web Crawler, Infoseek)	= Location & Access
Gopher, ftp	= Information Seeking Strategies Location & Access
Archie, Veronica	= Location & Access
Down/up load, ftp	= Use of Information
Web page creation (HTML authoring)	= Synthesis

Conclusion: A Computer at Home?

Computers can be powerful tools for helping kids solve information problems. When we look at computers and related technologies from a Big Six perspective, we see that computers can be used by students for more than just playing games. Computers make it easier for students to organize and present information for reports, papers, or even homework assignments (Synthesis). Computers connected to the Internet can help students communicate for Task Definition and receive feedback (Evaluation). Various CD-ROM databases and the Internet provide students with expanded Information Seeking Strategies. They learn to search electronically (Location & Access) and use information (Use of Information) through cut and paste, and downloading.

This brings us back to the question posed at the beginning of this chapter. Should parents buy a computer for students to use at home? Our answer is a qualified, yes.

Computers are productivity tools that boost students' skills in information problem-solving. Since the world relies increasingly on computers in all aspects of life, our children need to be more than familiar with them. They need to be regular, comfortable users of computers.

Students should use word processing, graphics, and other Synthesis tools on a regular, even daily, basis. They should be frequent users of a full range of electronic resources on stand-alone computers, on local area networks, and via the Internet. Using electronic information resources should be part of their Information Seeking Strategies. Location, access, and use of these electronic resources should also be commonplace. Today's students should be comfortable with communicating with others through e-mail and other electronic means.

The bottom line is that if students are to become proficient users of computers, they need regular and easy access. Computers need to be a part of their everyday lives either at school, in community settings, or at home. But computers are expensive. Low-end models cost around $1,000 and more powerful systems can easily run double that amount or more. Then, there's the added cost of a printer, modem for connecting to the Internet, and monthly connectivity charges. Software and electronic information resources can be expensive as well.

So, we say that if possible, parents should try to arrange to have a computer in the home with some basic capabilities: word processing, database/file management, graphics, and presentation software. Most of these functions are combined in the relatively inexpensive "works" programs (e.g., Clarisworks™ , Microsoft Works™). A printer is also desirable, but if necessary, students can print out their work in school. Your computer doesn't have to be the latest model with all the special features. But, we do caution against getting one that's too old. Older computers can be difficult to set-up and maintain, and the software programs may be very different from the ones that your children are using at school.

Internet access, while also desirable, is less crucial at this point in time. Students increasingly have access to e-mail and the World Wide Web through their school library media centers and sometimes even in their classrooms. And, as we stated earlier, WWW resources may not be as useful or as easy to find and use as other electronic information resources.

To use these other electronic information resources, we believe it's essential for students to become frequent users of school library media centers and public libraries. Libraries offer a wide and up-to-date array of information resources, and libraries expand students' views of the world of information. Therefore, for the home, we recommend only a limited set of electronic resources—an atlas, thesaurus, dictionary, and perhaps an encyclopedia. Sometimes these come bundled in one software package.

Some of these reference works can be purchased less expensively in their print versions (e.g., a current almanac).

Parents who do not have the means to purchase home computers can still help their children by seeking out alternative access to computers for their

---

Figure 4:

The Big Six Information Problem-Solving Process with Technology Tools

Big Six	Technology
• Task Definition:	electronic mail listservs, newsgroups problem-solving software
• Information Seeking Strategies:	online library catalogs magazine/newspaper indexes World Wide Web (WWW) Gopher full-text electronic resources
• Location & Access:	online library catalogs magazine/newspaper indexes WWW browsers (*Netscape, Microsoft Explorer*) WWW search engines (*Yahoo, Lycos, InfoSeek*) Archie, Veronica
• Use of Information:	cut/paste down loading up loading
• Synthesis:	word processing presentation software electronic spreadsheets database/file management systems Web page (HTML) authoring
• Evaluation:	electronic mail (e-mail) spell/grammar/style checkers

children in schools, libraries, and in the community. Regular, frequent, and easy access to computers is the important thing, not necessarily having them in the home. Schools and government agencies are increasingly aware of the importance of providing equal access to computers to all students. Some schools, libraries, and community agencies have special programs that provide extended hours of access to computers. Some even provide computers on extended loan to the home. Parents need to find out about these options. If none exist, they should raise questions as to why they do not.

Summary

This chapter focused on computer technology and the Internet:

(1) Technology can be a powerful tool for handling information problems in any work, school, or life contexts.

(2) Too often, technology is offered as a solution without a problem, or an answer in search of a question.

(3) The Big Six provides a framework for applying computers and the Internet to specific information problem-solving skills.

(4) Figures 2, 3, and 4 summarize the Big Six-technology connection. They show how the various technologies increase students' productivity in the various Big Six steps.

(5) By focusing on technology in the Big Six context, parents are really accomplishing something. We put our children in a position to be successful. We are giving them a competitive edge through technology.

(6) A home computer is desirable but not necessary. If they don't have a home computer, parents should ensure that their children have regular and frequent access to computers—through school, libraries, or other community agencies.

5

Assisting with Assignments

Examples from Various Subjects

In this chapter, we will show you in more detail how to use the Big Six with assignments in specific subject areas. We'll present a range of examples that model the approach you can use with your children. We do suggest that you read through all of the examples, regardless of subject area or grade level.

Many of the ideas we suggest for one subject area are also appropriate to use in other subject areas. The examples for elementary school may provide ideas for working with older children and vice versa. We will end the chapter with a brief discussion on how you can help your children when assignments are open-ended, vague or unclear.

Helping With Homework in Science

In the elementary grades, science is taught by topic or theme, for example, weather, plants, genetics or magnetism. In the higher grades, topics are grouped under the broad sciences of earth science, astronomy, biology, chemistry, and physics. In some science classes, the focus is on skills of investigation and inquiry that cut across various scientific disciplines. These skills include: observation, measurement, problem-solving and questioning.

In many schools, students still learn and practice science by listening to the teacher, reading the textbook, answering questions, and performing demonstration labs. In demonstration labs, students learn to observe, measure, and use scientific tools to study various topics. The combination of classroom experiences and homework assignments are intended to enable students to learn science concepts and skills and apply them to the range of science subjects.

From our experience with students, we believe the keys to helping students succeed in science is to help them:

- see the big picture—what the teacher is trying to accomplish.
- organize their science information for easy understanding and presenting back (on quizzes, tests, and assignments).
- learn new vocabulary words (crucial in biology, for example).
- learn the connections between vocabulary words.
- understand the general concepts before moving to the specifics.

Typical homework assignments in science are answering questions at the end of textbook chapters and writing up lab reports. Parents can help with these assignments by guiding students to make sure they:

- understand the actual question (Task Definition).
- know where to find the information to answer the question (Information Seeking Strategies).
- understand the material once they've found it (Use of Information).
- know the specific ways the teacher wants the answers to appear (Synthesis).

As we stressed earlier, the least helpful thing parents can do is give students the actual answers to homework questions. That's really "doing the homework for the students," and it doesn't help students develop their own science understandings or information problem-solving skills. If children get to the right section in their textbook or in their class notes and still have trouble understanding the material, that's a Use of Information problem. Parents can help their children here by explaining what the words mean or by showing them ways to organize the information (in charts or tables, for example). Parents might also help by arranging for extra help from school—not necessarily in science, but rather in reading and comprehension in science.

When we work with teachers, library media specialists, and administrators, we recommend they have students cite sources for every answer to every assignment. That means that at the end of a response to a question, students should put the source of information in parenthesis. For example, for the question, "How far is the sun from the earth?" the student might respond:

3. The sun is 93 million miles from the earth. (Science textbook, page 134)

A student might just as easily cite an encyclopedia, WWW site, another book (print or electronic), an expert, or even themselves, for example: (myself, February 15, 1996). Citing in this way helps us to check the students' Big Six Skills:

- Did they use an appropriate source? (Information Seeking Strategies)
- Were they able to locate the right section/page of the source? (Location & Access)
- Did they extract the right information from the section/page? (Use of Information)
- Did they organize and present the information in a way that makes sense or as required? (Synthesis)

Crediting sources in homework assignments also helps students establish good citing habits for more extensive reports, papers or projects. If teachers don't require citing in homework, you might suggest it to the teacher, or ask if it's OK for your children to do so. Of course, if your children feel uncomfortable doing something that no one else is doing, then back off.

Lab reports generally are required in secondary science classes, and often represent a significant portion of the course grade. Students can boost their science grades by completing all their lab assignments and doing so in the way the teacher wants them to. Amazingly, a number of students don't turn in all their science lab reports. Either they aren't able to follow the procedures, or they are unable to write up the report.

Parents can help by making sure that students understand that lab reports are an important part of their grade. You can also help by asking your child to walk you through the lab process in general or in relation to a specific lab. In this way, you'll be able to tell if the child understands the task and has a plan to complete the lab. It's very important to help students recognize exactly how their teachers want the lab report to be presented. Teachers have very specific ways they want labs to be carried out and reported, and the format is almost always the same from lab to lab. Following instructions and reporting the lab as the teacher requests is a relatively easy way to raise a science grade.

Computers can also help students complete science labs. Electronic spreadsheet software is very useful for organizing data, carrying out various mathematical formulas, and creating graphs and charts. Word processing makes it easier to do the lab report in the required format. Furthermore, once one lab is done, the word processing format can be retained for future labs.

Beyond traditional science homework and assignments, students have projects, demonstrations, and original experiments. These range from reports on animals, planets, and other science topics (generally in the elementary grades) to more sophisticated hypothesis-testing situations. Science report assignments encourage students to follow their own interests and learn more about a specific science area. Science reports also provide excellent opportunities for students to develop and practice their Big Six skills.

When students perform science experiments and do demonstrations, they integrate basic skills such as collecting, observing, measuring, classifying, and using special equipment like microscopes and meters with science content and concepts. For example, when students are assigned a project to gather a collection of leaves, label the leaves' characteristics and organize the leaves for presentation, they are using science skills to learn about science content. Here too, they are developing their Big Six skills.

Whether a science project is done by an elementary or secondary student, the criteria for success remain the same. What changes is the level of sophistication with which the students try to answer the question or solve the problem. For most science reports, experiments, and demonstrations, criteria for success include:

- choice of topic (interesting, unique, question-driven)
- following the scientific method
- clarity
- completeness
- proper documentation (supporting evidence).

We offer you the same recommendations for helping with science projects that we offered you for helping with other science assignments. Students need to do their own work, but parents can act as guides by asking key questions and helping their children understand the tasks and how they will proceed. Parents can also help by arranging for necessary equipment or resources (including computers), seeing that their children have access to the school library media center or public library, or by lining up extra assistance if needed.

Big Six Approach: The following steps in the Big Six approach are particularly valuable for helping students with science:

- Task Definition: to understand the requirements of the specific problem at hand—the homework, assignments, projects. This includes determining the types of information that will be necessary to complete the assignments.

- Information   to decide on the best approaches to gathering
  Seeking Strategies: information for assignments and reports and for collecting data for experiments and demonstrations.

- Use of Information: to understand and use science vocabulary comfortably.

- Synthesis: to organize and present science information in the most appropriate formats (as would scientists): structured lab reports charts and graphs posters, models or demonstrations written reports.

Sample Science Assignment:

Adam is a tenth grade student studying about mold and spores in biology class. His homework assignment is to complete an independent science project. The teacher tells the class that they must compare two ways to grow mold on food to verify the conditions that are best for growing molds: warm and damp or cool and dry. Students have two weeks to complete their experiment.

Parents' Role: Some Ways Parents Might Help

BEGIN **BEFORE**

Task Definition:
- If Adam is unsure about how to begin, ask him to explain exactly

what he thinks the teacher expects him to do and what he thinks he will find. Sometimes it helps to sketch out the experiment on paper.
- Discuss the conditions of the experiment (comparing two conditions: warm and damp versus cool and dry).

Information Seeking Strategies:
- Help Adam realize that he doesn't need any additional information resources beyond the experiment itself.

Use of Information:
- Discuss how he will observe the experiment. What will he observe? Will he measure anything? How will he take notes? Will he set up a chart in advance? How often does he plan to observe?

Synthesis:
- Following the decisions about note-taking, talk about alternative ways to organize the data.
- Discuss how a computer might be used to help out.

Evaluation:
- Discuss how Adam will know when he is done.

DURING

Use of Information:
- Ask how Adam is going to see if there are any problems. If there are problems, brainstorm alternatives.

Evaluation:
- Check to see if Adam thinks the project is going to be completed on time.
- Offer to proofread the final report.

AFTER

Evaluation:

- Ask Adam what he would do differently if he could do the assignment again.

Helping With Homework in English/Language Arts

Understanding language and communicating thought in words is essential to all aspects of academic and personal achievement. The ability to use and create language are crucial skills because of their importance to one's total educational program, and of course, to one's success in life. School assignments in all subject areas require the competent use of language arts skills. Some schools use the term English, others use "Language Arts" to describe the school subject that focuses on reading and communication skills, and on experiences with literature, film and other communications forms.

Reading is central to success in school. Students who are "readers" perform better in their course work and on all forms of assessments (Krashen, 1993). The ability to read for information, whether it be in a short story, novel, or biography, or in a science or social studies textbook, is an indicator of achievement.

Communication skills—writing, speaking, and presenting information using various media formats—are fundamental to the successful completion of homework, assignments, and tests. When students are asked to express ideas in essays, letters, short answers, research reports, speeches, drawings, photographs, multimedia shows, or WWW sites, they are learning and practicing skills they will use for a lifetime.

English/Language Arts is taught in many different ways. Traditionally, teaching reading skills involved the use of special textbooks called "readers" that relied on a phonics or a sounding out approach. More recently, we hear about "whole language," a reading approach that emphasizes learning to read in context. In whole language, students read text books and other reading materials as opposed to readers. Contrary to some current criticisms, true whole language does include a phonics program at primary levels. Whether called "whole language" or not, your children are likely to be in reading programs that include both phonics and exposure to a wide range of children's books and media.

Grammar, vocabulary, spelling and writing fundamentals are also taught in a combination of ways. Many schools still rely on some form of English textbook, but students also receive lots of experience with "real world" materials, for example literature, newspapers, and magazines. Schools have expanded teaching communication beyond writing by including film, video, and other multimedia forms. Even in early elementary school grades, students are learning to use computers to create multimedia presentations that combine sound, images, and video along with text.

Literature instruction too has expanded beyond simply reading and discussing fiction, poetry, and essays. Students now explore a geographically and culturally diverse range of creative works. They also experience many different media formats for the presentation of creative work.

In our experience, the way to help students succeed in English/Language Arts is to help them:

- see the big picture—what the teacher is trying to accomplish.
- understand the format the teacher is looking for (for example, letter, essay, multimedia show), and make sure they know how to present in that format.
- understand the structure of good writing and presenting.
- read/experience for content—be able to pull out the key ideas from writing and media presentations.
- build their vocabulary—use interesting words in interesting ways.
- organize their information for easy understanding and presenting back (on quizzes, tests, and assignments).
- use proper grammar, spelling, and punctuation—in written and multimedia presentations.

Some of these points are similar to the points we emphasized for helping students with science. That's because while there are some unique ways for helping with each subject, there are also some general ways we can help that cut across all subjects.

Typical homework assignments in English/Language Arts are writing/presentation exercises, vocabulary and spelling words, worksheets, and reading comprehension exercises. Parents can help with these assignments by guiding their children to make sure they:

- understand the specific assignment (Task Definition).
- know where to find the information for the assignment (Information Seeking Strategies).
- understand the material once they've found it (Use of Information).
- know the specific ways that the teacher wants it presented (Synthesis).

Writing for English/Language Arts can be different from writing for science or other subjects. For example, science generally requires a direct, methodical writing style. English/Language Arts writing can be more creative and unique. Some English/Language Arts programs emphasize "writing in the subject areas." Interestingly, it's OK to write up "what you didn't find" in science. You might describe an experiment that resulted in "no findings." In English, that's not acceptable. A student wouldn't write a book report about what she thought a book was going to be about, but later turned out to be about something else.

Computer technologies are increasingly important for presenting information. Word processing is now considered a basic writing tool. Parents must find ways for their children to have regular and easy access to computers for word processing. Besides the help it provides for composing and editing, word processing provides spelling and grammar checking functions. These functions don't spell and write for the students, but they do highlight where the student might have made a mistake. Students learn some writing rules by interacting with spelling and grammar checkers. Even if they don't know how to use these programs, parents can help their children by helping them to focus on the purpose and message of the presentation.

Students are often asked to write papers and reports for English/Language Arts. Usually these are tied to some specific subject content, for example, writing about authors, illustrators, or some form of literature. However, sometimes reports are assigned to "teach students library or information skills." We certainly believe in the importance of library and information skills—that's what this book is all about. However, students learn these skills best when they are linked to real content. Open-ended reports that allow students to choose any topic of interest can be more difficult than reports tied to specific subject content.

Fortunately, the Big Six approach can help whether the report or paper is specific or open-ended. The Big Six provides a framework for each step in the creation of the report. Parents can help their children by (1) making sure they understand the overall process and (2) checking to see if they are having difficulty with any specific step.

We find that task definition can be a big problem for students, especially if the writing topic is open. Students may select a broad area to write about, but it's often too unfocused or unformed. Parents can help their children by just talking about the topic. What are the possibilities for study? What questions would students like to answer in the report? The most successful reports go beyond merely describing a topic. They have direction, consider certain questions, maybe even test a theory or hypothesis. For younger children, posing interesting questions can accomplish this. Older students should be encouraged to develop a thesis statement.

For example, suppose students choose to do a report on whales. One approach would be to describe whales, their features, habits, etc. This is a typical descriptive report—the kind you might find in an encyclopedia. In fact, that's what students may have in mind because that's what they are most familiar with. An alternative would be to consider important questions: Are whales threatened? Are they better off today than 25 years ago? Is pollution hurting whales? A thesis statement might be, "There is no longer a threat to whales." This type of approach forces students to look for specific types of information and to synthesize in unique ways. It also provides excellent opportunities for students to develop their Big Six skills.

There's another pitfall to watch for in papers and reports. Students may decide on a topic and feel pretty good about it. Then they go to the school library media center or public library, look around and declare, "there's nothing in there on my topic." It's common for some students to give up at this point and pick another topic. What we see here is a typical problem in Information Seeking Strategies and Location & Access. The library is much more than just the book collection. Too often, kids check the library catalog, can't find a book listed under the narrow topic they search, and then give up. Kids need to consider all the possible resources in the library where they might find useful information. The library includes electronic and print books, magazines, references, newspapers, WWW sites, people and much more.

Students also need to consider different approaches for searching for specific resources and for information within those resources. This involves using various subject terms, synonyms, and the commands of different access systems. Sound complicated? It is. But, library media specialists and public librarians are eager to help. One of the best things you can do for your children is to make them feel comfortable about asking librarians for help.

Parents can provide guidance in every step of the Big Six process while students work through their reports and papers. But, parents must avoid the temptation to do the work for the children. We've seen too many situations where it's the parent that goes to the library, uses the access tools, finds the resources, and makes copies of the relevant sections for the children. Sometimes parents even help organize the overall paper. This really doesn't help the kids because the kids don't get the chance to develop their own information skills.

Big Six Approach: There's a natural connection between information skills and English/Language Arts. For example, the criteria used by many teachers to determine a student's ability in English/Language Arts include:

- organization of ideas
- use of facts and opinions
- clarity of ideas stated
- proper grammar, spelling and punctuation.

The Big Six approach can help students with these and other English/Language Arts criteria, for example:

- Task Definition: to understand the requirements of the specific problem at hand—the homework, assignments, paper or report. This includes developing a focus, key questions, or thesis.

- Information
  Seeking Strategies: to consider a wide range of resources.

- Use of Information: to be able to read for a purpose—to quickly recognize the valuable sections.

- Synthesis: to write in the appropriate style for the task—to use correct grammar, cites, and bibliography.

- Evaluation: to check grammar and spelling before turning in an assignment.

Knowing whether to point out or correct grammar and spelling errors is a dilemma for many parents. Too often, the "battles" over grammar and spelling become the focus of parent-student interaction. We certainly don't want our children to turn in work that has errors. At the same time, we don't want to spend all our time on the technical details or in confrontation. While students may need assistance with grammar and spelling, they may have far greater needs in task definition and synthesis. Therefore, think about helping with spelling and grammar in terms of the overall circumstances—what are the most important needs of your children?

Of course, the ideal situation is for students to check their own spelling and grammar. One way to encourage this is to have students use the spell and grammar checkers that are part of most computer word processing programs. These checkers don't correct the text for the student, they simply point out possible errors for the student to consider. Another way to encourage good grammar, is to have the students talk about what the teacher expects of them. If they identify grammar and spelling as part of what makes a good assignment, you can follow-up with discussing ways of helping them to check and, if necessary, learn the proper rules.

Using the Big Six itself may help with spelling and grammar. The Big Six approach emphasizes a logical process and having students take control over their own work. Using the Big Six reinforces students routinely checking their assignments before turning them in. By learning and using the Big Six, students are more likely to think about Evaluation concerns—such as checking spelling and grammar.

Finally remember that in some situations, teachers may not require 100% accuracy in terms of grammar and spelling. As much as this may go against our own instincts, there's probably a good reason for this. If you are concerned, talk to the teacher about it—find out their motivations. This is consistent with the overall Big Six approach—determining what's required of students and helping them to succeed.

Sample English/Language Arts Assignment:

Maria is in first grade. Her teacher gives her a homework assignment that requires her to make an ABC book. In addition to writing the book, she must share it with the class.

Big Six Approach: From a Big Six view, there are many different ways that Maria might complete this assignment. Here is an example of what Maria might do, but please remember that this is only one possible approach.

- Task Definition: After the teacher explains the assignment, Maria decides that she will make an ABC book based on the topic of food. In talking with her mother, she realizes she will need to gather lots of names of foods (and spellings).

- Information Seeking Strategies:

  Maria decides to ask her mom for help in getting information about foods. Together they realize that a cookbook might help and that maybe she can find one for kids in the library media center.

- Location & Access:

  The library media specialist helps Maria to find a children's cookbook.

- Use of Information:

  Maria reads through the book to find the names of fruits, vegetables, and other foods. She writes each food name on a card.

- Synthesis:

  Maria uses pictures from magazines, construction paper, and crayons to illustrate her book. She puts all the pages in alphabetical order and staples them together. Maria practices reading her ABC book to her mother.

- Evaluation:

  Maria decides that she likes her book, but that coming up with an idea for the letter "X" was hard.

Parents' Role: Some Ways Parents Might Help

BEFORE

Task Definition:

- Ask Maria if she knows what she's supposed to do. Don't settle for a "yes or no" answer. Have her explain the assignment in her own words.

- Talk about what information she will need (for example, the names of foods and their spellings).

Information Seeking Strategies:

- Brainstorm together all possible information sources to find the names and spellings of different foods.

Use of Information:

- Suggest that Maria keep track of all the food names and spellings. Explain how putting each food name on an index card might be helpful.

Synthesis:

- Ask Maria to describe what the ABC book will look like when she is done.

DURING

Location & Access:

- Give Maria some old magazines and suggest that she cut out pictures of food.

Synthesis:

- Encourage Maria to use her own ideas and imagination to illustrate each food.

AFTER

Evaluation:

- Ask Maria what she liked most about making the book, and what she might do differently next time.

Helping With Homework in Math

In mathematics, the goals are for students to learn basic and advanced operational concepts and to develop computational skills. Students should also be able to apply their math skills to problems. Math instruction is generally topic-driven. In elementary schools, students seek to master various math topics from simple arithmetic operations (addition, subtraction, multiplication, division) to fractions/percents and simple geometry. Secondary school math instruction can include logic, algebra, geometry, statistics and probability, trigonometry, and calculus. State and district guidelines and students' abilities and interests determine the specific math courses taken at the upper secondary level. Problem-solving is also considered an important component of elementary and secondary math programs.

Computing is also part of most math programs. Computer math curricula include programming (even at an early age), applications programs such as electronic spreadsheets and databases, and the theories and concepts behind computing. Of course, computing is not usually limited to the math curriculum. More and more schools are integrating computing into every subject area and many use computers for information through the library media program. We encourage you to contact your child's school to learn more about their approach to computers and technology.

Math instruction is fairly straight-forward. Teachers explain concepts and demonstrate how to solve various math problems. Most often, teachers use a math textbook and/or handouts. Students work through problems and practice number and word problems for homework.

In traditional math instruction, the topics are covered in sequence and generally follow the textbook. In high school, students take a full year course in a major math topic, for example geometry in one year and trigonometry the next. Today, it is also common for schools to take a more integrated approach. Teachers cover a number of math topics each year, increasing the complexity as students progress.

Just because math instruction is straight-forward, it doesn't mean that it must be dull or uninteresting. Many teachers make math exciting and capture students' interests by making math relevant to the students. These teachers continually relate math skills and concepts to real world examples through actual practice and through computer programs and simulations.

Parents can also help make math easier for students to learn by helping them:

- see the big picture—what the teacher is trying to accomplish.
- see how the specific math topic might be used in real settings.
- match the math problem at hand to problems in the textbook or class notes.
- have the necessary tools to complete the math work (for example, calculator, tables, protractor, compass).
- match the math problem at hand to problems in the textbook or class notes.

In our experience, the last point is the most important. In math, students learn formulas, operations, and facts. But all of these are meaningless unless students know when to apply them. Parents can make a big difference here by helping students match their knowledge and skills to specific problems. In most cases, this means finding a model answer that matches the problem the students are working on.

When parents are confronted with children who are having trouble with math, they usually try to "teach" the children how to do the problem. This approach rarely works. The students become frustrated because "that's not the way my teacher showed me how to do it." But they really don't remember just exactly how the teacher did it. The parents get frustrated because they are just trying to help (and they too may be struggling a bit to remember how to do the problem). And the whole thing escalates—sometimes into a major blowup.

The alternative is for the parent and child to work together to find the teacher's model for the math problem. In Big Six terms, this is an Information Seeking Strategy concern and then a Location & Access concern. What are all possible sources for models? How about class notes, the textbook, staying after school and meeting with the teacher, my friend and classmate, Jennifer Johnson. Now, which of these sources is the best?—it's the model the teacher uses and the one that's easiest to access. There's no single right answer all the time. For some students and classes, the answer will be the textbook. For others, class notes are the key. Just realizing where the appropriate information can be found can do much to ease the situation.

Big Six Approach in Math:

While deciding on the best source for math information is a crucial application of the Big Six approach to math, it's not the only one. Students should also focus on:

- Task Definition: to determine what is expected, for example, translating word problems into numbers and symbols. Also recognizing the type of problem and the matching model needed.

- Information Seeking Strategies: to decide the possible and best sources to use for specific problems and for the entire school year. Some teachers rely on the text book others ignore the text (except for practice questions) and expect excellent class notes.

- Use of Information: to read and comprehend graphs.

- Synthesis: to show all work to present problems and answers in the format desired by the teacher.

- Evaluation: to formally check all answers.

Sample Math Assignment:

Joanne, a tenth grade student, is working on probability problems from her math book. For homework, she is to complete questions 1-3-5-7-9-11 on page 116 in her math textbook. But Joanne was sick earlier in the week and missed two days of school.

Big Six Approach: Using a Big Six approach, Joanne can try different things. Here is an example of what she might do. Again, please remember that this is only one possible approach.

- Task Definition: Joanne realizes that because she missed school, she doesn't really know how to do the assigned problems.

- Information   Joanne asks her older brother what she
  Seeking Strategies   should do. He asks what the teacher relies on most—the textbook or class notes. Joanne says that class notes are most important.

- Location & Access: Joanne calls her friend Tonya and arranges to go over to her house to look at her notes.

- Use of Information: Tonya explains how the notes are organized and shows Joanne the pages that specifically relate to the homework. Joanne copies Tonya's notes.

- Synthesis: Joanne is able to do three of the problems, but gets stuck on the other three. She writes a note on her homework that she needs additional help.

- Evaluation: Joanne realizes that she still needs direct information from her teacher and arranges to come in for extra help.

Parents' Role: Some Ways Parents Might Help

BEFORE

Task Definition:
- Discuss with Joanne what she might have missed while she was absent.

Information Seeking Strategies:

- Discuss alternative sources for finding out what she missed and how she can get the needed information.

Location & Access:

- Drive Joanne over to her friend's house to borrow her notes.

Evaluation:

- Discuss whether she will need additional assistance.

DURING

Use of Information:

- Ask how it's going—are there any problems? If there are, brainstorm alternatives.

Synthesis:

- Offer to explain to the teacher that Joanne attempted to do the homework.

Evaluation:

- Discuss how Joanne intends to get additional assistance.

AFTER

Task Definition:

- Ask Joanne if she's made plans to get additional assistance.
- Discuss if she has any other concerns about the math assignment.

Evaluation:

- Ask Joanne what she found most helpful about Tonya's notes or other forms of assistance.

Helping With Homework in Social Studies

Mention social studies and many students will groan. In spite of the fact that people talk about politics and various aspects of society everyday, the study of history and societies in schools doesn't always inspire interest and excitement. So, part of the challenge in applying the Big Six approach to social studies includes helping to make the connection between students' everyday lives and social studies.

This need not be as hard as it sounds. We all tune in to the news in one form or another—on radio or television, by reading newspapers, by talking to friends, or even by surfing the Internet. Talk to your kids about what's going on in the world and in the neighborhood—what's interesting to you. Ask them what they are studying in social studies and make the link to current events. Almost every day, there's something in the news that may relate to what they are studying. When students begin to make the connection between their own interests and social studies, they are motivated to learn more. The connections will also help when they are faced with defining topics and important questions for essays, reports, and projects.

In school, social studies is taught either as a sequence of historical events or as an interactive set of topics and concepts. Teachers also seek to de-

velop such skills as interpretation, analysis, and application. A typical social studies question asks students to "compare and contrast" events,
people, or cultures. For example, elementary students might be asked to
compare and contrast their community with other communities in the
United States. A secondary topic might be to compare and contrast two
forms of government.

In the early grades, social studies topics include neighborhoods and communities, holidays, careers, the United States, and countries of the world.
Secondary curriculum encompasses the study of United States and world
history and culture as well as topics in sociology, psychology, and econom-
ics.

Parents can help with social studies just by making the link between what's
going on every day and students' social studies work. Parents can help students to succeed by helping them:

- understand key terms and concepts.
- see how specific social studies ideas fit into the larger picture of a
  general topic and the overall social studies area.
- recognize the difference between fact and opinion.
- recognize the difference between generalizations and specifics.
- be able to provide examples of historical events or important
  concepts.

Big Six Approach: In social studies, the Big Six approach can help students
focus on:

- Task Definition: to key in on the intent of a question or
                       assignment. There are also different forms of
                       questions, and students can learn to recognize
                       various forms in order to provide appropriate
                       responses.

- Information
  Seeking Strategies: to consider the widest possible range of sources and then select the most appropriate source for a particular need.

- Use of Information: to be able to pull out relevant information for a specific need.

- Synthesis: to organize information for easy reporting. To use timelines, graphs, charts and other formats for presenting historical and social science information accurately and in a way that makes sense.

Sample Social Studies Assignment:

Leon, a seventh grade student, is required to do a social studies report on the topic of recycling. He is supposed to use library media resources (including the Internet) for his information. He will be required to make a three-minute oral class presentation using visual aids. Leon has one week to complete the assignment.

Big Six Approach: Here is a Big Six example of what steps Leon might go through. As we noted in earlier examples, please remember that this is only one possible approach.

- Task Definition: Leon decides to narrow the topic of recycling to an investigation of ways to recycle tires.

- Information
  Seeking Strategies: Leon talks to the school library media specialist about his idea. She suggests using CD-ROM magazine indexes and searching the World Wide Web as two good sources.

- Location & Access: Leon searches using the Magazine Articles Summaries CD-ROM and also searches the WWW using Yahoo.

- Use of Information: Leon reads the articles on the screen and is able to cut and paste directly into his word processor.

- Synthesis: He practices his presentation. He makes a few changes in order to be more specific about the benefits of recycling tires.

- Evaluation: Leon reviews his draft and realizes he has plenty of specific information on recycling tires, but needs to add more general information about recycling in the introduction.

Parents' Role: Some Ways Parents Might Help

BEFORE

Task Definition:
- If Leon is having trouble narrowing the topic, ask him what he already knows about recycling. Then, brainstorm together some specific questions that relate to what he knows about the topic of recycling tires.

Information Seeking Strategies:
- Remind Leon that the assignment requires him to use the library media center.
- Encourage Leon to ask the library media specialist for information rather than exploring around the library by himself.

Use of Information:
- Remind Leon that keeping track of where he gets his information (so that he can properly cite his sources) will save him time and effort later.

Synthesis:
- Offer to listen to the report when Leon gets ready to practice.

Evaluation:
- After listening to Leon practice his oral report, ask him what he thought the best part of the report was. Ask him to think about one thing he could do to improve the report.
- Inquire about the presentations of the other students in Leon's class. Ask what made their presentations interesting and what he learned from them.

Helping with Homework in Other Content Areas

The examples and subject areas we have talked about in this chapter certainly do not cover the whole range of school curricula and corresponding Big Six applications. In school, students gain valuable knowledge and skills in health, music, art, home and careers, physical education, business, technology, reading, and other subject areas. The techniques and strategies outlined and discussed in this chapter are applicable to all these areas. We encourage you to help students with homework and assignments by helping them to see how the Big Six approach is applicable to any subject area or personal decision.

Throughout this book we have emphasized six basic skills (the Big Six) you need to consider when you help your children with homework and assignments. Though the subject matter and topics may change, it's important to remember that the process and skills required for success stay the same.

To help your children in any subject area, focus on the assignment and try to think about where your children are likely to have difficulties. Do they fully understand the assignment (Task Definition)? Do they know how they will be graded? Do they know what the most important parts of the assignment in terms of grading are (Evaluation)? What about sources for information required to complete the assignment? Do your children understand what information will be needed? Do they have some good sources to check out first (Information Seeking Strategies)? Will they be able to read and comprehend the material in the resources? Will they be able to pull out relevant information easily (Use of Information)? Are they clear about what their final presentation will look like (Synthesis)? You can help identify possible roadblocks and help students move through them.

Very often, students have assignments that are not clearly stated. These assignments seem to create a lot of stress for students and their parents. How should you deal with assignments which appear to be vague or open-ended? We will end this chapter with some suggestions that will help you whenever you are faced with this situation.

Vague Assignments—How to Help with Vague, Confusing or Open-ended Assignments

By vague or open-ended assignments, we mean assignments that are very general in nature. These assignments usually require students to make choices about the topic and about the way of presenting the results of their work. Many reports and projects fall under this category. In most of these cases, teachers are trying to motivate their students by encouraging them to tap into their own interests and allowing them to choose "any topic they want" or "any special focus within a broad topic." Unfortunately, the result is often the opposite. Students become confused or anxious because they really aren't sure what they have to do. We've seen students in all grade levels face this situation.

Here's an example—eighth graders working on reports on "current events" are asked to select any current world or United States issue, explain it, and take a stand. Some students will agonize over what topic to choose. They will have difficulty thinking of anything interesting (to them) or they will try one topic after another or they will simply put off deciding at all. Carol Kuhlthau's research (Kuhlthau, 1993) shows that most students have feelings of uncertainty when they first get a task. Once they select a broad topic area, they feel better—even optimistic.

Once students decide on a general topic (say censorship), they will begin to narrow the focus. Here, Kuhlthau says, students can become confused, frustrated, and doubt themselves. For example, they might go to the library media center or public library and look in the catalog for "censorship." If they find something, they might be all right. But many students run into problems here. They don't find anything in the catalog. The books aren't on the shelves. There's too much information. They are faced with hundreds of resources on the World Wide Web. At this point, many students retreat. They go back to the last time they felt good—back to selecting a topic. Some students go 'round and 'round—selecting a topic, getting frustrated in the search process, and coming back to selecting a new topic.

This frustration can also continue even after the students push through and collect the information they need. They are relieved and pleased with themselves for gathering the necessary information, but they again become confused and doubtful when they face the task of extracting the relevant information and organizing the report. The open-endedness or vagueness of the assignment (for example, you can present in any format you want) only adds to the frustration. This situation is not limited to reports, papers, and projects. Students can experience the same bewilderment with vague or confusing homework assignments.

The solution to these dilemmas is not for parents to ask the school for detailed, step-by-step assignments. Certainly, there are times when teachers need to be more specific and directive, but we want our children to assume responsibility for their own work. We want them to become "independent learners." That means they must first realize that vague assignments are their problem not the teacher's. If students don't fully understand what's expected of them, they will be the ones to suffer (with poor grades, for example) not the teacher.

Independent learning doesn't mean that students do it all on their own. It does mean students should take charge of the problem. If students don't understand the specifics of a task, they need to seek clarification and assistance. Certainly, this might mean asking the teacher, but it could also mean talking with classmates, parents, library media specialists, other teachers, or other students who have taken the class. It might mean looking carefully at the assignment as written or initially explained, brainstorming options and selecting those that seem best. It might involve looking at similar assignments that were given in previous years.

Most teachers are eager for students to take charge of their own work. They encourage students to ask questions and seek assistance. However, if your children are reluctant to do so, or if they are in a situation where a teacher isn't open to giving assistance in these situations, then you and your children need to think about alternatives and decide on the best courses of action. This might mean deciding to use one of the alternative ways of seeking clarification mentioned above. Or it might mean the student needs to push ahead and learn how to approach a certain type of teacher. Or you may decide that in this case, it is necessary for you as a parent to get involved.

However, we cannot emphasize enough that the important issue here is for students to accept the assignment as their own and move ahead. Of course, we believe that the Big Six Skills approach can be an effective tool to use when students are faced with vague assignments. Attention to three of the Big Six can make a big difference when students have trouble understanding what's really important:

- Task Definition: what the task is, the various parts, and the apparent options.

- Evaluation: the teacher's criteria for earning a good grade.

- Synthesis: how to best organize and present the solution/information.

Parents can help focus students' attention on these skills and they can guide students through the entire process. We will conclude this section with a breakdown, by Big Six skill, of the kinds of questions and actions that you can use to help guide your children through vague, open-ended or difficult assignments.

Task Definition:

Do you understand the purpose of the assignment?
What are the questions you are trying to answer?
Can you break down the assignment into parts?
Can you determine the types of information needed?

• *Encourage children to ask for help!*

The classroom teacher, library media specialists, other teachers, other students, or other students who have taken the class can be useful sources of information when an assignment is unclear or difficult to understand.

Teachers want students to be successful, and they want to help. Often they don't realize that students need help unless the students ask.

• *Look over the assignment sheet with the student.*

Sit down with your child and try to outline together what the teacher expects. Focus your attention on what is required. If your child is unsure about what is required, you might suggest that he or she bring in an outline or restatement of the assignment and have it confirmed by the teacher. This will ensure that students are on the right track before they invest a lot of time and energy.

• *Have the student write out questions about the assignment for the teacher.*

This strategy, similar to the one above, will allow students to determine what they know and what they don't know about the assignment. A good list of questions will provide a solid basis for a student-teacher discussion.

• *Call or send a note to the teacher.*

Sometimes it is appropriate for a parent to become more directly involved. Direct communication by parents to teachers can help clarify the teacher's expectations. Most teachers appreciate the opportunity to talk to parents.

┌ Information Seeking Strategies: ─────────┐

What do you already know about the topic?
What are some possible sources you can use?
Which might be the best sources of information?

• *Brainstorm a list of possible information sources.*

Brainstorming and narrowing is a very useful process. Students often need help in determining not only the full range of possible information sources, but also which are the best to use.

• *Encourage students to seek assistance from the school library media specialist.*

School library media specialists are trained professionals who have expertise in the entire information problem-solving process. They are especially good at helping students develop Information Seeking Strategies.

• *Have students consider other specialists, professionals, or community members.*

Public libraries are excellent sources of information. Other good resources are often only a telephone call or an e-mail message away. Generally, students are warmly received by both private and government agencies that are happy to provide lots of good information for students to use in projects and reports. Community members often appreciate the opportunity to help students be successful.

Location & Access:

Do you know where to find the sources you need?
What are some key words for searching for information in sources?

• *Encourage students to take advantage of school library media centers.*

The library media center is the information center of the school. The professional library media specialist builds collections specifically targeted at the curriculum and assignments. Materials in the library are organized for easy location and access. Sources include not only books and audio visual materials, but also electronic information that can be easily accessed from CD-ROM or the Internet.

• *Use libraries yourself.*

The public library is the information center of the community. Students learn best by example. Studies show that kids who use libraries frequently have parents who are regular library users.

• *Brainstorm key words to try when using various access tools—catalogs, indexes, databases, table of contents, appendices, and glossaries.*

Students sometimes miss valuable information in sources. They can also waste a lot of time and effort trying to locate needed information. Not only do students need to know about indexes and special access tools, but they need to be able to think of a range of key words to use when searching for information. Parents can help by explaining about key words and synonyms, and by working with students to help them think up key words for the particular assignment. A thesaurus is also a useful tool here.

> ## Use of Information: ──────────
>
> Do you understand the information in the sources?
> Can you pull out what you need from the resources
> to answer the question?

• *Check to see if the information is understandable.*

Particularly with open-ended assignments, students may find information resources that are written beyond their reading level. Parents can help here by reading a source with their children or by helping to define difficult terminology.

• *Help children understand charts, graphs, and other visual material.*

Often information is organized in charts and graphs. Some students have difficulty using information when it is presented graphically. You might want to have your child try to explain what the chart or graph represents and how the information is organized. You might also need to "talk through" a chart or graph and explain what it means to you.

• *Help children with note taking methods.*

Note taking is an important skill. Many schools still teach the "note card" method for writing notes from information sources on individual 3x5 cards. But, most people in college or business use a photocopy machine to copy the relevant pages and then highlight the relevant sections. If the teacher requires students to use the note card method, go with that. If that's not specifically required, you can help by encouraging your child to try the photocopy-highlight method. The important issue here is for you to help your child recognize and highlight the valuable sections. (You can also help by providing change for the copier).

┌ Synthesis:

Are there specific requirements for presenting the
information?
If so, do you know how to present in this way?
If not, what are you planning to do to present the
assignment results?
Are you clear about how to organize all the information you have?

• *Discuss what students are expected to hand in to their teacher.*

In order for students to do well in school, they must be able to organize
and present their homework and assignments in the format their teacher
expects. The format for a science lab report is different from the format
for an English short story or a math proof. You can help your children
understand these differences so they will make their presentations according to their teachers' expectations.

Vague assignments are often open-ended in terms of presentation expectations. For example, students may be told that they can "do a paper, or
create a model, video, multimedia show, etc." While this may seem to give
students lots of options, it can also be very confusing for them. Parents
can help here by helping their children evaluate the options in terms of
format, effectiveness, time, and effort. Students and parents can discuss
the choices and make decisions.

• *Show some different ways to organize the information.*

Synthesis begins with the organization of information to meet the task.
There are different ways to organize. We can, for example, organize as a
story (by time), in categories, alphabetically or by number. Students sometimes have difficulty knowing where to begin. Parents can help by talking
through some organizing options. Having students describe or even draw
a chart showing what they intend to do can make a big difference.

Evaluation:

Is the assignment complete—not just finished?
Did you check your answers to make sure that you
    answered the question completely?
Did you take into consideration how the assignment
    will be graded?
What did you do that worked out particularly well—
    and that you would recommend to someone else?
If you could change one thing, what would it be?
Do you have time to do so?
What could you do better the next time you have
    a project like this?

• Check to see if the student has completed the assignment.

Asking, "Is the assignment completed?" is different from asking "Are you are finished?" Students may be finished even though the assignment is not done. Parents can help their children check to see whether they've done all parts of the assignment. For open-ended assignments, this is particularly important because while there may be only a few guidelines, they count a lot.

• Ask if there's one thing to do that would make the assignment better.

This is really part of ongoing Evaluation. Students should continually check to see how well they are progressing with all the tasks of the assignment. As they approach the end of an assignment, they should be able to think about one or two more things they could do to make it better. Perhaps it's checking the spelling one more time. Maybe it's adding to one section. Maybe it's adding a chart or a graphic. These additional changes can make the difference between just getting by and doing a solid job.

The final Evaluation check should always be comparing the result to the original task as defined.

• *Make sure students understand when the assignment is due.*

Students often lose some of the credit for an assignment because they turned their work in late. Parents can help by discussing ways to keep track of deadlines and by encouraging students to meet them. Parents can also discuss examples of how meeting deadlines is important in work and at home. Parents can also model how they make sure they meet their own deadlines.

• *Look to the future—try to get students to think about what they might do differently next time.*

We know that getting kids to look beyond the project they are currently working on isn't always easy. But, the more you can do to get them to think about how they could do a better job as well as save time and effort, the better it will be for future assignments. That's what learning is all about. Try to keep the discussion positive, but see if you can get your children to talk about what they will do to make their work even better next time.

Students should also reflect on the parts of the assignment that went particularly well. This might have involved choosing an interesting topic, using a really good source, or presenting the information in an exciting way. Although some students may have negative feelings about schoolwork, parents can help them recognize areas for improvement and build the student's self esteem by highlighting their strengths. Students should have pride in their work, and parents can help them to do so.

Summary

Homework and assignments are given in all subject areas. Assignments are ways for students to show teachers what they know, but they are also ways for students to learn, review, remediate, or extend subject matter taught in the classroom. Let's review the major points we covered in this chapter:

(1) Typical assignments include: reading, short written essays, projects, worksheets, and completing questions from the back of a text book.

(2) Parents can help their children with any type of assignment. They can help any time in the assignment process—before, during, and after.

(3) Many of the techniques and suggestions described for a particular subject area can also be helpful with assignments in other subject areas.

(4) When parents help their children with the Big Six process, they help them become independent and successful—able to complete almost any assignment effectively and efficiently.

(5) One of the best ways that parents can help is to encourage students to assume responsibility for their assignments—not to wait for the teacher to tell them what to do.

6

Bringing It All Together

A Parent Conversation with Mike and Bob

By now, you probably have lots of ideas about how you might better help your children succeed. The Big Six offers a framework you can use to guide your children through assignments and homework, and also help them solve problems and make decisions.

We consider being able to work with information an important key to success in school and beyond. Parents can do a great deal to help their children use information in effective and efficient ways. We hope our approach and the discussion presented in this book have given you lots of practical ideas about how you can help your children succeed. We also hope we've given you the confidence to go ahead and try things out.

We are sure you have questions and concerns as well. There's no way for us to answer your specific questions in this book format, but we can try the next best thing. We can have someone ask questions for you.

We will conclude this book with a parent "sitting in" for you, conversing with Mike and Bob. If we don't cover your specific questions, we encourage you to imagine what we might say based upon what you've already read. And, you can always write or e-mail us at the addresses listed in the back of this book.

The Conversation

Parent: When I read through the book, it all makes sense. But I'm really not sure it will work with my own kids. What can I do? How do I start?

Mike: My advice is to jump right in and give it a try. Start small. Try to help with Task Definition. If you can get kids to rephrase the assignment in their own words, that's a big step. Try to make sure they really understand what's expected of them.

Bob: Ask them to tell you how they think they are going to be graded. Have them be the teacher for a moment. What's most important to me, the teacher? What am I going to be looking for? In what form do I expect the work?

You also said you were uncertain if it's going to work. Are you working with your kids now? If so, how's it going?

Parent: Yes. I do work with my children, especially my youngest. She's in fourth grade. My biggest problem is getting her to do her homework in the first place. How do you handle that?

Bob: Well, some kids put off doing their homework because it's such a chore. They don't quite "get it." It takes a long time and they don't get much positive feedback from their teachers. Doing homework or assignments seem like big, overwhelming tasks. You can help them to see that it's manageable and doable. First, ask them to lay out the tasks as we suggested in the book. Jump to synthesis and discuss how the final product will look. Then move back to Information Seeking Strategies—not just brainstorming resources, but deciding quickly which resources are best to use. At this point, your child has a plan—what to do, how it will look, what information to use. The "battle" is more than half won.

Remember how you felt when you were given a difficult homework assignment? Well, your kids probably have the same feelings of anxiousness and insecurity. When they feel anxious, they are likely to find excuses for not doing their work. So, as a parent, you have to make them feel secure enough so that they can do the assigned homework. They need to feel that it's doable—maybe with a little bit of direction—but in the end they can and will be able to get it done.

Mike: The Big Six approach can help you to figure out where the problem is in relation to doing the homework. By working with your children, you should begin to realize where they are having the most difficulty. Is it really in Task Definition, or are they unable to understand or comprehend the textbook? That would be a Use of Information problem, and you could focus more specifically on that, or seek specific assistance from the teacher or school. Identifying and resolving difficulties in the homework process may remove some of the barriers that may be the reasons why your daughter doesn't want to do her homework.

Of course, there may be bigger issues going on here as well. We aren't psychologists or counselors, and we don't say that the Big Six is the answer to all problems. If you have continual, serious problems, and you've tried our approach, we urge you to speak with the professionals in the schools.

Parent: No, I don't think there's a major problem here. I just think she's a little bit lazy.

Bob: Well, everyone approaches things a little differently. And that's OK as long as she fully understands her responsibilities and meets them. As we've emphasized, the Big Six is not a linear, in order process all the time. Some kids like to follow the process one-by-one, but others jump around. Again, that's OK. But to succeed, they have to do each step at some point. If she appears lazy, it may be because she has problems somewhere in the process and is reluctant to do the work. By working through the Big Six, you can help sort this out.

Mike: Again, I want to stress remembering how it felt for you to be a kid working on school assignments. There's always that dread you felt when you were first confronted with homework or a task. Putting yourself in your children's shoes is a good idea. Look at the situation from their perspective.

Parent: Another question. This approach seems okay for younger kids, but what about my teenager? How does it work for older kids?

Mike: Information problem-solving is for everyone. As we say in the book, whether we are aware of it or not, we go through the Big Six process every time we solve an information problem or make a decision based on information. I've taught the Big Six to every age group—from kindergarten to elementary to secondary to college to adult. It offers something to everyone.

Bob: However, just like in science or in reading or in mathematics, we don't teach the same things in the same way to all age groups. In the early grades, we seek to build up students' skills and our involvement is likely to be more direct. When we work with older kids, we want them to be more independent. Hopefully, they have learned some of the skills already. So, the challenge is to help them identify their weaknesses and help them overcome them. So when we work with older students, we act even more as a guide, trouble-shooting and using the Big Six as a model.

I also find that older students' needs often relate to Task Definition and Evaluation, and sometimes Synthesis. Their tasks are getting more complex and they need to spend time really figuring out what they need to do. They also need to have a clear idea about how their results will be judged. Synthesis is also important because they are expected to have more sophisticated presentations—the quality of their writing, for example.

Mike: Remind students to think about what made them successful on previous assignments. That's Evaluation too.

Parent: OK, thanks. That makes sense to me. Now I have a question about technology. I really don't understand this stuff. How much do I personally need to know? Also, I'm worried about getting ripped off.

Bob: First, find out what's happening in your school regarding computers. What are your children already doing? What does the school expect the children to be doing in a year or two? If you don't understand computers yourself, then you need to be in contact with the teachers. The school library media specialists are also really good sources of information about technology in the schools.

Mike: Right. You don't have to be an expert on computers to help your kids. In fact, many kids know more than their parents or teachers when it comes to computers. But we adults generally know about when and how to apply computer skills to get things done. The entire chapter on technology explains how computers can be used for information problem-solving. Even if you don't know how to use computers, you can help your children determine exactly what they need a computer to do.

Bob: For example, do they need to use a word processor to write better papers? Do they need to use e-mail to communicate with teachers and classmates about an assignment? Or do they need to locate a NASA space experiment on the WWW for science class? You can help your children focus on their needs for computers without being an expert yourself.

Parent: So, do we really need to buy a computer for the house?

Bob: We could hedge, but the answer is yes, if at all possible. Students benefit from having a computer at home because using computer tools can become part of their everyday life. You don't need to buy the most expensive, high-end model. A moderate-range computer that will run baseline software or an integrated package of word processing, electronic spreadsheet, database management, graphics, and telecommunications is sufficient. We think a computer is today's equivalent of yesterday's pad and pencil.

Mike: And don't forget to get a printer. Most people who don't also get a printer when they buy their computer are sorry and have to make another trip to the store. Today, you can usually get a package deal that includes a computer, printer, monitor, modem, CD-ROM drive and baseline software. In terms of brands and such, you may need help in picking out a system. This is an information problem, right? Brainstorm the different Information Seeking Strategies available to you—a friend who seems to be an expert, a book or magazine on computers, someone at the school or library. Then decide which of these sources seems the best for this particular task.

Bob: But if you can't afford a computer, remember that there are other opportunities for students to gain access to computers. As we said in Chapter 4, you can seek out alternative opportunities in libraries, schools, and community agencies. The important thing is for you to take an active role in making sure that your children have regular and frequent access to computers. Don't just assume that there's enough access provided in school.

And by the way, learning to use computers is a good chance for you to change roles with your children. Have them teach you how to use the computer. This builds a learning environment in your home.

Mike: Yes. We do encourage you to learn some baseline computer skills yourself—word processing, use of CD-ROM information resources, maybe even exploring the Internet. Having your children teach you is a terrific way to begin and get used to working together.

Parent: That's enough about technology. I have another question. In the book, you comment about task definition and having the children go back and talk to the teacher if they are confused or unsure. That's easy to say, but it's not easy for many students to confront their teacher. What can they really do if they get a confusing assignment?

Mike: First, it's not a confrontational thing. We've worked with thousands of teachers, and believe me, they want your children to succeed. Teachers are in a tough situation. They are dealing with lots of different children each day, each with unique problems and concerns. They're also responsible for a wide range of curricula as well as lots of extra-class matters. The sheer volume of tasks can be overwhelming.

The bottom line is that teachers want your students to do well. That's why they became teachers. When students succeed, that reflects well on the teachers. So, most teachers would welcome students raising questions. I'm a teacher, and although I try to give clear directions about assignments, my students sometimes get confused. Just like me, I believe that most teachers would be receptive to students asking them questions to clarify what's important and necessary for an assignment. I look at questioning as an opportunity to teach and learn, not as a confrontation.

Bob: Right, but it can still be intimidating for the student. There are a number of things you can do to help your children with this. Have them go back to the teacher at your request. Something like, "I tried to explain the assignment to my Mom, but I had trouble. She asked me to go over it with you so I could explain it to her." You can also write a short note to the teacher explaining the situation and asking for clarification. The students and the teacher need to see that seeking clarification on an assignment is valuable. It's part of learning.

Parent: But what if the teacher really is unapproachable?

Bob: Well, in that case, we need to consider other Information Seeking Strategies. For example, the kids can talk to other kids about the assignments. What does everybody think the teacher seems to want on assignments? Does your child know anyone in the class who always does well? What about talking to a student who had that teacher in the past?

Mike: And, of course, if there are continual difficulties, a parent-teacher conference may be necessary. There's a major emphasis today on the home-school relationship. The United States Department of Education's *Strong Families, Strong Schools* (1994) publication and other studies show that parental involvement is crucial. So, you are likely to find a much more welcoming attitude in schools today. Parents and teachers are working hard to cooperate, not confront.

Bob: But, it's still better if the student is the one taking the lead and the responsibility. We want students to realize that it's in their best interest to clearly define the task. They are the ones who will benefit—in terms of better grades, saving time and effort, and being able to succeed at whatever they wish to do.

Parent: One last question. You are certainly convincing about the Big Six. But really, just how important is it? Isn't this just part of every subject?

Bob: Information skills aren't optional. They are essential. You've heard the hype—we live in an information age, an information society. Well, it's true. In an information society, information skills are basic skills. And we want to do more than just have kids survive in this information age. We want them to thrive. Information seeking, communication, and decision-making skills are vitally important if we are to be successful, not just for the future, but for today.

Mike: Information problem-solving is the new literacy. Being able to read is not enough. People must be able to process and interact with a range of technologies and a range of information formats. Being able to write is not enough. People must be able to present their ideas using and combining a range of media. Being able to do simple mathematical computations is not enough. People must be able to understand numerical information presented in various formats and be able to use technology for organization, manipulation, and presentation of numerical data.

Bob: As far as being part of every subject—absolutely. That's what we've been saying in this book. The Big Six approach to information problem-solving is applicable across all subject areas and situations. Parents can help their children to succeed by using the Big Six Skills approach and related tools to help their children learn, achieve and be successful.

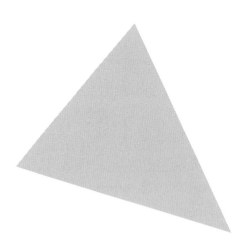

Do you have further questions or comments? Mike and Bob are interested in hearing from you. They can be reached at:

Mike Eisenberg
ERIC Clearinghouse on Information & Technology
Syracuse University
4-194 Center for Science and Technology
Syracuse, New York 13244-4100

E-mail: mike@ericir.syr.edu

Bob Berkowitz
ERIC Clearinghouse on Information & Technology
Syracuse University
4-194 Center for Science and Technology
Syracuse, New York 13244-4100

E-mail: reberkow@mailbox.syr.edu

References

Dempster, F. N. (1992, summer). Using tests to promote learning: A neglected classroom resource. *Journal of Research and Development in Education, 25*(4), 213-217.

Jansen, B. A. (1995). *Big Six assignment organizer.* (Available from Barbara A. Jansen, Librarian, Forest Creek Elementary, Round Rock I.S.D., Round Rock, TX 78664 512-464-5358 bjansen@tenet.edu).

Krashen, S. (1993). *The power of reading: Insights from the research.* Englewood, CO: Libraries Unlimited.

Kuhlthau, C. C. (1993). *Seeking meaning: A process approach to library & information services.* Norwood, NJ: Ablex.

Moles, O. (1996, August). *Reaching all families: Creating family-friendly schools. Report.* <http://www.ed.gov/pubs/ReachFam/index.html> (version current at 10 Oct., 1996). Produced in collaboration with the Partnership for Family Involvement in Education and the U.S. Department of Education.

Paulu, N.; Perkinson, K. (Ed.) (1995, September). *Helping your child with homework: For parents of elementary and junior high school-aged children.* Office of Educational Research and Improvement: U.S. Department of Education. Also available at Internet WWW page URL: <http://www.ed.gov/pubs/parents/Homework/index.html> (version current at August 1996)

Smith, C. B. (Developer). (1996). *Parents as tutors: Helping with homework* [Video]. (Available from EDINFO Press, P. O. Box 5247, Bloomington, Indiana 47407).

Survey shows half of American homes have computers or will buy one soon. (1995, August 1). Sample issue. *Education Technology News, 12*(16), p.126.

U. S. Department of Education. (1994). *Strong families, strong schools: Building community partnerships for learning.* A research base for family involvement in learning from the U.S. Department of Education. Washington, DC: Author. (ED 371 909)

Appendix

Appendix A:
Big Six© Assignment Organizer

Name: _____ **Teacher:** _____

Fill out Big Six #1-5 <u>before</u> you begin to work on your assignment. Fill out Big Six #6 <u>before</u> you turn your assignment in to your teacher.

Big Six #1: Task Definition

What am I supposed to do?
What information do I need in order to do this?
1.
2.
3.
4.
5.
6.

Big Six #2: Information Seeking Strategies

What are the possible sources to find this information?	Which ones are best for me to use?

Big Six #3: Location and Access

Where will I find these sources?	Who can help me find what I need?

Big Six #4: Use of Information

How will I record the information that I find?	How will I give credit to my sources?
___ take notes using cards ___ take notes on notebook paper ___ take notes using a data chart ___ draw pictures ___ talk into a tape recorder ___ other _____	___ write title, author, page number on note cards ___ write title, author, page number on notebook paper ___ write title, author, page number on data chart

Big Six #5: Synthesis

What product or performance will I make to finish my assignment?	How will I give credit to my sources in my final product or performance?
	___ include a written list (bibliography) ___ after the performance, tell which sources I used ___ other _____

Big Six #6: Evaluation

How will I know that I have done my best? (all must be checked before assignment is turned in)

___ what I made to finish the assignment is what I was supposed to do in #1

___ information found in #4 matches information needed in #1

___ I gave credit to my sources (even if I used a textbook)

___ my work is neat

___ my work is complete and includes my name and the date

©Eisenberg/Berkowitz, 1990. Organizer ©Barbara A. Jansen, 1995.

Appendix B:

Applying the Big Six to Sample Homework Assignments

Information Problem-Solving Process	1st Grade Language Arts—Maria's assignment is to make an ABC book.	
Task Definition	After the teacher explains the assignment, Maria decides that she will make an ABC book based on the topic of food. In talking with her mother, she realizes she will need to gather lots of names of foods (and their spellings).	
Information Seeking Strategy	Maria decides to ask her mother for help in getting information about foods. Together they realize that a cookbook might help and that maybe she can find one for kids in the library media center.	
Location & Access	The library media specialist helps Maria to find a children's cookbook.	
Use of Information	Maria reads through the book to find the names of fruits, vegetables, and other foods. She writes each food name on a card.	
Synthesis	Maria uses pictures from magazines, construction paper, and crayons to illustrate her book. She puts the pages in alphabetical order and staples them together. Maria practices reading her ABC book to her mother.	
Evaluation	Maria decides that she likes her book, but that coming up with an idea for the letter "X" was hard.	

7th Grade Social Studies— Leon is required to do a three minute oral report about recycling. His presentation should include visual aids.	10th Grade Math— Joanne is working on probability problems from her math book. She missed two days of school this week.
Leon decides to narrow the topic of recycling to an investigation of ways to recycle tires.	Joanne realizes that because she missed school, she doesn't really know how to do the assigned problems.
Leon talks to the school library media specialist about his idea. She suggests using CD-ROM magazine indexes and searching the World Wide Web as two good sources.	Joanne asks her older brother what she should do. He asks what the teacher relies on most—the textbook or class notes. Joanne says that class notes are most important.
Leon searches using the *Magazine Articles Summaries* CD-ROM and also searches the WWW using *Yahoo*.	Joanne calls her friend Tonya and arranges to go over to her house to look at her notes.
Leon reads the articles on the screen and is able to paste directly into his word processor.	Tonya explains how the notes are organized and shows Joanne the pages that specifically relate to the homework. Joanne copies Tonya's notes.
He practices his presentation. He makes a few changes in order to be more specific about the benefits of recycling tires.	Joanne is able to do three of the problems, but gets stuck on the others. She writes a note on her homework that she needs additional help.
Leon reviews his draft and realizes he has plenty of specific information on recycling tires but needs to add more general information about recycling in the introduction.	Joanne realizes that she still needs direct information from her teacher and arranges to come in for extra help.

from Eisenberg/Berkowitz, *Helping With Homework* © 1996

Appendix C:
Big Six Skills Overhead Transparency Masters

The Big Six

2
Information Seeking Strategies

- What are possible sources?

- Which are the best?

The Big Six

3

Location And Access

- Where is each source?

- Where is the information in each source?

I know!

The Big Six

4

Use Of Information

- How can I best use each source?

- What information in each source is useful?

The Big Six

5

Synthesis

- How can I organize all the information?

- How can I present the result?

Permission is granted for educational use or reprint of these overhead transparency masters as long as the authors are properly and prominently credited.

Information about the availability of the Big Six Skills overhead transparencies, bookmarks, and posters can be obtained from the ERIC Clearinghouse on Information & Technology, Syracuse University, 4-194 Center for Science and Technology, Syracuse, New York 13244-4100; (315) 443-3640 or 1-800-464-9107.

The Big Six

6
Evaluation

- Is the task completed?

- How can I do things better?

Appendix D:
Big Six Skills Bookmark

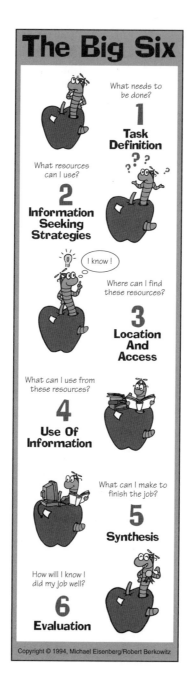

Appendix E:

What is ERIC? (Educational Resources Information Center)

ERIC, the Educational Resources Information Center, is a national education information system sponsored by the Office of Educational Research and Improvement in the U.S. Department of Education. The main product of ERIC is a bibliographic database containing citations and abstracts for over 950,000 documents and journal articles published since 1966. Most of the document literature cited in ERIC can be read in full text at any of the 900+ libraries or institutions worldwide holding the ERIC microfiche collection. In addition, users can purchase copies of ERIC documents from the ERIC Document Reproduction Service. Journal articles cited in ERIC can be obtained at a subscribing library, through interlibrary loan, or from an article reprint service.

How do I find information in ERIC?

The ERIC Database can be searched manually through its two print indexes, Resources in Education (RIE) and Current Index to Journals in Education (CIJE). Over 3,000 libraries and information centers subscribe to one or both of these monthly indexes. The database can also be searched online: (a) through a computer based information retrieval service (b) by CD-ROM or (c) on a locally mounted system, which may be accessible through the Internet. Online searching is an expedient way to access many years' data, to locate items on specific topics, or to find items meeting several criteria at once. The number of libraries offering online and CD-ROM search services is rapidly increasing.

What is ERIC/IT?

The ERIC Clearinghouse on Information & Technology, or ERIC/IT, is one of 16 clearinghouses in the ERIC system. It specializes in library and information science and educational technology.

ERIC Database

ERIC/IT acquires, selects, catalogs, indexes, and abstracts documents and journal articles in these subject areas for input into the ERIC database.

Among the topics covered in library and information science are:
* management, operation, and use of libraries and information centers
* library technology and automation
* library education
* information policy
* information literacy
* information storage, processing and retrieval
* networking

Topics covered in educational technology include:
* design, development, and evaluation of instruction
* computer-assisted instruction
* hypermedia, interactive video, and interactive multimedia
* telecommunications
* film, radio, television, and other audio-visual media
* distance education
* simulation and gaming

What else is available from ERIC/IT?

Each year, ERIC/IT publishes Monographs, Digests, and Minibibliographies in the fields of educational technology and library and information science. Our semiannual newsletter, ERIC/IT Update, announces new clearinghouse products and developments, and ERIC/IT Networkers provide helpful information for using ERIC-related resources on the Internet.

Publications
- Digests—provide brief overviews of topics of current interest and references for further reading
- Monographs—feature trends and issues analyses, synthesis papers and annotated ERIC bibliographies
- ERIC/IT Update—a semi-annual newsletter

User Services
- Responds to inquiries about ERIC and matters within the ERIC/IT scope area
- Workshops and presentations about ERIC and database searching
- Assistance in searching the ERIC database

AskERIC
- Internet-based question answering service for educators
- AskERIC Virtual Library, an Internet site of education-related information resources including lesson plans, InfoGuides, listservs and much more.

E-mail: askeric@ericir.syr.edu   Internet: http://ericir.syr.edu
Gopher: gopher ericir.syr.edu

Would you like to submit your work to ERIC?

Have you written materials related to educational technology or library and information science that you would like to share with others? ERIC/IT would be interested in reviewing your work for possible inclusion in the ERIC database. We actively solicit documents from researchers, practitioners, associations, and agencies at national, state, and local levels. ERIC documents include the following and more:

- Research Reports
- Program Descriptions
- Instructional Materials
- Conference Papers
- Teaching Guides
- Opinion Papers

How do I find out more?

For additional information about ERIC or about submitting documents, or for a current publications list, contact:

ERIC Clearinghouse on Information & Technology
Syracuse University
4-194 Center for Science and Technology
Syracuse, New York 13244-4100
Michael B. Eisenberg, Director
Telephone: (315) 443-3640, (800) 464-9107 Fax: (315) 443-5448
E-mail: eric@ericir.syr.edu;
Internet: http://ericir.syr.edu/ithome

Questions about the ERIC system can also be directed to:

ACCESS ERIC
1600 Research Boulevard
Rockville, Maryland 20850-3172
Telephone: (800) LET-ERIC
E-mail: acceric@inet.ed.gov

ERIC Clearinghouses

- Adult, Career, and Vocational Education
- Assessment and Evaluation
- Community Colleges
- Higher Education
- Disabilities and Gifted Education
- Languages and Linguistics
- Reading, English, and Communication
- Science, Mathematics, and Environmental Education
- Urban Education

- Elementary and Early Childhood Education
- Counseling and Student Services
- Information & Technology
- Educational Management
- Rural Education and Small Schools
- Teaching and Teacher Education
- Social Studies/Social Science Education

Support Components
- ERIC Document Reproduction Service
  Telephone: (800) 443-ERIC

- ERIC Processing and Reference Facility
  Telephone: (301) 497-4080

Helping with Homework

Selected ERIC Bibliography

ERIC Documents

Eisenberg, M. B. & Berkowitz, R. E. (1990). *Information problem solving: The Big Six skills approach to library and information skills instruction.* Norwood, NJ: Ablex. Ablex Publishing Corporation, 355 Chestnut St. Norwood, NJ 07648 ($22.95). Document not available from EDRS. (ED 330 364)

This book presents a systematic approach to integrated library and information skills instruction that is based on six broad skill areas necessary for successful information problem-solving otherwise referred to as the "Big Six Skills." It begins with definitions and explanations of the Big Six Skills approach, moves to a discussion of implementation, and concludes with specific exemplary instructional units and lessons. Six chapters emphasize practical and tested techniques to develop and implement library and information skills instructional programs based on the Big Six Skills approach: Chapter 1 revisits the overarching concepts and themes of the approach; chapter 2 defines and explains an expanded view of the specific levels of the Big Six Skills; chapter 3 provides contextual examples and exercises to develop a better understanding of the Big Six Skills; chapter 4 focuses on practical actions that relate to planning and implementation of the approach; chapter 5 offers exemplary instructional units to act as models for elementary and secondary settings; and chapter 6 provides examples of generic lessons that can be adapted to assist in delivering the desired integrated instruction. Two appendixes include completed exercises from chapter 3 and four sample curriculum maps generated from a K-12 sample curriculum database. A subject index and a 27-item bibliography are also provided.

Indiana State Department of Education. (1990). *Get ready, get set, parent's role: Parent booklet.* [Booklet]. Indianapolis, IN: Author. (ED 337 264)

This handbook for parents stresses the ways in which children benefit when the responsibility for education is shared by the school and the home. The first section of the handbook proposes that parents' attitudes and their relationship with their children may be the most influential factors in children's success in school. It further proposes that the home setting should be a learning environment that helps children develop good study habits. The second section encourages parents to model active learning by reading aloud to their children. Several children's books at various reading levels, 24 children's magazines, and 6 resources on parent involvement, are suggested. The third section discusses practical activities that can be done at home or in other family settings to help children succeed in school. An extensive list of such activities is provided.

Konecki, L. R. (1992). *Parent talk: Helping families relate to schools and facilitate children's learning.* Paper presented at the Annual Meeting of the Association of Teacher Educators (Orlando, FL, February 17, 1992). (ED 342 745)

"PARENT TALK" is a newsletter distributed to approximately 10,000 recipients of Aid to Families with Dependent Children in Grand Rapids, Michigan, along with their assistance checks. The newsletter is designed to help parents relate to schools in order to facilitate and promote their children's success. Five topics are discussed: (1) what PARENT TALK is; (2) how PARENT TALK originated; (3) the theoretical background and its importance as related to teacher education; (4) preliminary results of a survey that indicate how PARENT TALK recipients feel about it; and (5) future directions for PARENT TALK. A figure shows representative samples from PARENT TALK dealing with parent-teacher conferences and how to get the most from them; listening skills and ways to encourage good listening habits; and discipline tips. Although the long-term continuation of the project is unknown, response data from recipients indicate that PARENT TALK is a useful tool which has helped link parents and educators for the benefit of children. Four appendices include a PARENT TALK survey, PARENT TALK Issue Topics, a PARENT TALK order form and a questionnaire to schools and agencies.

Lankes, R. D. (1996). *The bread & butter of the Internet: A primer and presentation packet for educators.* (IR-101). Syracuse, NY: ERIC Clearinghouse on Information & Technology. (ED number pending)

Written for educators, this book provides simple explanations for using Internet resources like e-mail, listservs, telnet, ftp, gopher and the World Wide Web. Internet addresses are provided for many popular professional educational resources. This book also features a teacher training presentation packet, complete with 45 overhead transparency masters and presentation notes. You can use this book and presentation packet to bring others up to speed on Internet technology too.

Periodicals

Eisenberg, M. B. & Berkowitz, R. E. (1992). Information problem-solving: The big six skills approach. *School Library Media Activities Monthly, 8*(5), 27-29,37,42. (EJ 438 023)

Eisenberg, M. B. & Berkowitz, R. E. (1995, August). The six study habits of highly effective students: Using the Big Six to link parents, students, and homework. *School Library Journal, 41*(8), 22-25. (EJ 510 346)

Presents the "big six," problem solving strategies of highly effective students in all grade levels and subject areas. Outlines steps parents and media specialists can follow to help students with their homework.

Sidebars present the big six skills and information seeking activities and a big six assignment organizer for grades three through five.

Explains the components of a library and information skills curriculum and integrated instructional model that was developed to help students solve information problems. The six steps include (1) task definition, (2) information seeking strategies, (3) location & access, (4) use of information, (5) synthesis, and (6) evaluation.

Eisenberg, M. B. & Spitzer, K. L. (1991, Oct.) Skills and strategies for helping students become more effective information users. *Catholic Library World*, 63(2), 115-120. (EJ 465 828)

Addresses the implications for education of the expansion of information technology and proposes a model for teaching information skills within the context of an overall process. A model called the "Big Six Skills" is presented, and its application to information problems related to school, life, and work are explained.

Granowsky, A. (1991). What parents can do to help children succeed in school. *PTA Today*, *17*(1), 5-6. (EJ 436 757)

A national survey of elementary and middle school principals examined how parents can help children succeed academically. Principals recommended that parent behavior support children's self-esteem. The same scale is reprinted for parents to complete and compare their responses with those of the principals.

Scarnati, J. T. & Platt, R. B. (1991, Oct.) Lines and pies and bars, oh my! Making math fun. *PTA Today*, *17*(1), 9-11. (EJ 436 759)

The article discusses strategies for parents to help their children improve math skills. It examines graphing skills and looks at three types of graphs (line graph, bar graph, and pie chart). Various simple activities illustrate what all scientists and mathematicians do when conducting experiments or developing mathematical models.

Van, J. A. (1991, Oct.). Parents are part of the team at Hearst Award Winner's school. *PTA Today, 17*(1), 7-8. (EJ 436 758)

Discusses the programs, activities, and philosophies of a Missouri elementary school principal who became the National PTA's Phoebe Apperson Hearst Outstanding Educator for 1991. The principal encourages parents to spend time at school with their children; he stresses high self-esteem and community and family involvement.

How to Order ERIC Documents

Individual copies of ERIC documents are available in either microfiche or paper copy from the ERIC Document Reproduction Service (EDRS), 7420 Fullerton Road, Suite 110, Springfield, VA 22153-2852. Some documents are available only in microfiche. Information needed for ordering includes the ED number, the number of pages, the number of copies wanted, the unit price, and the total unit cost. Sales tax should be included on orders from Maryland, Virginia, and Washington, DC.

The prices of paper copy are based on units of 25 pages (and/or any fraction thereof) at the rate of $3.97 per unit. The prices for microfiche are based on the number of microfiche for each document. The price for one to five microfiche for a single document is $1.34 (up to 480 pages).

Please order by ED number, indicate the format desired (microfiche or paper copy), and include payment for the price listed plus shipping. Call EDRS at 1-800-443-ERIC (or 703-440-1400) for information on shipping costs and/or other services offered by the contractor. Inquiries about

ERIC may be addressed to the ERIC Clearinghouse on Information & Technology, 4-194 Center for Science and Technology, Syracuse University, Syracuse, NY 13244-4100 (800-464-9107), e-mail eric@ericir.syr.edu; or ACCESS ERIC, 1600 Research Boulevard, Rockville, MD 20850 (800-LET-ERIC), e-mail acceric@inet.ed.gov.

Index